18
Doors

A Journey through Life and Death Row

Jack "BroJack" Williams

18 DOORS: A JOURNEY THROUGH LIFE AND DEATH ROW

ISBN: 978-0-9892436-0-5 (paperback)

Library of Congress Control Number: 2013906150

Printed in the United States

Second edition 2015

DEDICATION

I dedicate this book to my grandmother, Hazel Johnson, my two sons, Jason and Brandon Williams, and my good friend, Pastor Vic Bass.

18
Doors

A Journey through Life and Death Row

Jack "BroJack" Williams

ACKNOWLEDGEMENTS

I want to thank my two sons, Brandon and Jason, for giving me the most joy that this old world has to offer. Without Brandon by my side for the last seventeen years, I do not think I would have made it this far. Without Jason, my life would be incomplete and filled with an empty void. Thank you, my sons.

I also want to thank my grandmother, Hazel Johnson, who unfortunately passed away before she could see me as a Christian and now as an author. Without her love, I would not have survived.

Special thanks to Alan Mikolaj, who was very helpful in editing and formatting this book. Alan is an accomplished author whose latest book, *A Travel Guide to Leadership*, is a very informative and inspirational guide on how to be a leader in all aspects of your life.

Also special thanks to Shelley Terry and Janet Engquist for their proofing and editing assistance as well as my dear friend Deborah Lynn Horne for all her hard work.

Finally, to the man who was instrumental in helping change my life back in 1996, Bro Vic Bass. I would like to think that I would have found my Lord and Savior Jesus Christ eventually on my own, but I doubt it. Thank you, Bro Vic, for sticking with me, when all others left.

Contents

INTRODUCTION

DEATH CHANGES EVERYTHING

The Lord is close to the brokenhearted and saves those who are crushed
in spirit.
~ Psalm 34:18 ~

I really did not know what to expect as I slowly walked up to the casket that held the body of my little brother, Wayne. I was only twelve years old and this thing called "death" was new to me. Only days earlier, I was playing army in our neighborhood with my little brother, who was seven, never once thinking that soon I would be looking down on his lifeless body.

He was crossing the street in my hometown when he was killed by a drunk driver. My little brother was following my mother without her knowledge early on a Sunday morning when a man who had been drinking all night struck him and dragged his body under his car for two-hundred feet before he realized what he had done. My brother was not killed instantly but rather suffered for days in the hospital before his little body died.

It did not seem possible. His little face looked so peaceful lying in that big coffin. Everyone in the funeral home was crying and shouting hysterically. I tried to cry like everyone else because at the time, it seemed like the thing to do, but I could not muster one tear. This was not real and soon I would wake up from this nightmare. Well, it has been over forty years and I can relive that moment, standing beside my dead brother, as if it were yesterday. I can still smell the flowers. There is a distinct odor about funeral flowers. It is sort of a sweet-musty sickening smell, which stays with you the rest of your life.

After the shock of his death began to subside, then the bitterness and hatred began to set in. The pain of that loss was overwhelming. I started shutting down my emotions at that point, because if I ever lost another loved one again, I did not want to feel that kind of pain. I could not endure that again!

I believe that it was at this point I began to dislike my own mother, maybe even hate her, because deep down inside, I blamed her for not protecting my little brother. I never told anyone that because I lived in a family where the only time any emotions were shown was in tragedy. If the truth were known, at the time I wished I were looking at my dead mother, instead of my dead brother. Based on things I had seen her do up to that point in my short life, I felt like she probably deserved it more. I was positive my little innocent brother did not deserve to be lying in this big lousy casket. I was mad and things were about to get worse.

Eight years later my mother was murdered. She was shot through the head while sitting at a stoplight in her car. By the time I got to her funeral, there was nothing left inside of me to mourn her death. Drugs, alcohol, and violence had already taken over my life and it was just a matter of time until I got my turn in the casket. I think deep inside, I was silently looking forward to it. My brother and mother looked so peaceful in death. Maybe it was not so bad.

BROJACK

Before I go any further let me introduce myself. My name is Brother Jack "Brojack" Williams and today I am a minister of the Gospel of Jesus Christ. I am a graduate of Liberty University (Jerry Falwell started this university) and an ordained minister with a Certificate of Ordination and a Certificate of License. That means I am licensed to preach and teach the Gospel, perform marriages, administer the Sacraments, and to direct other functions of the ministry.

Earlier in my Christian life, I was an associate pastor at a church until God called me into evangelism ministry. When I resigned from my church, I had no idea what I was going to do, only that I needed to step out in faith and let God guide my steps — and guide my steps He did!

Currently, God has me involved in a prison ministry that has led me to death row in the state of Texas. For the past two and a half years, I have been visiting the most active death row in the country, ministering the Gospel of Jesus Christ whenever and to whomever I can. I have met and interacted with over 200 (of more than 300) inmates currently housed there. Out of these visits, Brojack Ministries was born. This ministry's primary purpose is to spread the Gospel (the good news) of Jesus Christ.

When God informed me that my next assignment was to spread His Gospel to convicted murderers, I had a big problem with that. It seems like I have been surrounded by death most of my life.

Besides the deaths of my little brother and mother, I later found my stepfather dead of a massive heart attack. I have buried my grandmother, who essentially raised me, and another brother named Rocky, who died a horrible death of heat exhaustion. Now God has me going into a place that is consumed by the smell of death. How can that be? Why would He do that to me? The horror of my own mother's murder still haunts me and now God wants me to tell convicted murderers how they can be saved!

Death row definitely lives up to its name. It is all about death! The men who I talk to weekly are responsible for the death of another human being and, in some cases, multiple human beings. The act of murder affects far more people than just the victims and their assailants.

The families on both sides are forever scarred. There is no getting over the horror of having a loved one murdered. You can only learn to live with it. Almost daily, I think about my mother and it has been decades since she was murdered.

Since I began my visits to death row, there have been thirty-one men executed by the state of Texas. I knew every one of them. Some I became very close to and some not so close, but by the grace of God, I have been able to share the Gospel of Jesus Christ with each one of them. That is only a fraction of the 496 men who have been executed in Texas since they reinstated the death penalty in 1972.

I call this book *18 Doors* because from the time I enter the main door to the prison, I must pass through eighteen doors until I am in front of a death-row inmate's cell door. I am not talking about doors that are opened by turning a knob; each one is controlled and opened electronically by prison guards. I go nowhere unless they open the door to let me pass. At times, I am surrounded by general population (G-pop) inmates who could harm me in any way they wanted before I could be rescued. About halfway through my journey through those doors to get out of death row, there is a big sign on one of the doors that says, "NO HOSTAGES BEYOND THIS POINT". That means that if I am taken hostage, they will not let me or the inmates out of that prison. If the inmates choose to make it so, I am a dead man.

This book is about my life's journey, a journey that has led me to become a preacher of the Gospel of Jesus Christ and to sharing that Gospel with murderers, like the one who murdered my brother and mother. Why would I open up my life to a world that may or may not care about anything that has ever happened to me or about anything I have ever done?

I think because I have been through so many things in my life and been in so many unique situations, I believe that many people will be able to relate to me and my ministry. I have done so many things that I am not proud of and have even landed in jail myself many times.

Maybe, just maybe, the readers of this book can compare their situation with one of mine and know that there is hope. I am living proof that you can survive the many tragedies and hardships of this world. How have I survived? How did I become the person I am today? How do I go into death row and witness to convicted murderers? The answers lie in the pages of this book.

Please join me on this journey. In the *first* section of this book, you will learn about my life, and how I have survived it so far. In the *second* section, you will learn how my life changed from evil to goodness. In the *third* and final section, you will learn about the lives of convicted murderers on death row in the State of Texas and how the path they choose in this world cost them everything. This section will read more like a diary as I document my interactions each visit until the inmate is executed.

Finally, maybe because of the time I have spent on death row, I can get some peace and closure on the murder of my brother and mother and in turn, help those of you out there who have had someone close to you murdered. You may possibly have a little better understanding and obtain some small measure of peace and closure as well.

It is my prayer that all who read this book will be blessed.

PART I: THE LIFE AND TIMES OF BROJACK

Before I formed you in the womb I knew you, and before you were born I set you apart; I appointed you as a prophet to the nations.

~ Jeremiah 1:5~

Chapter 1

The Tragedies of Life

I have told you these things, so that in me you may have peace. In this world you will have trouble. But take heart! I have overcome the world.

~ John 16:33 ~

Jesus knew that we would all face troubles and tragedies in this world and His words in the Bible verse above are meant to comfort us in these times. My life has been full of trouble and tragedies almost from the beginning and I feel I need to tell you about them so that you can understand how much of a miracle it is that I am now a preacher and that I currently witness to death-row inmates.

A DIFFERENT CHILDHOOD

I was born and raised in a small town in the Appalachian Mountains. It is almost the spitting image of Mayberry, North Carolina. That was the little town that Andy Griffith and Barney Fife lived in, as depicted in the *Andy Griffith Show*. It aired on television in the 1960s and you can still see the reruns on television today.

We had a two-lane main street running through the middle of town. On one side of the town was a large river and on the other side were tall mountains. The river was used to move coal from the coal mines to the train depots for delivery throughout the country. My hometown was exactly one mile in length from one end to the other. There was one stoplight in the upper end and one in the lower end. As I think back on it now, it was actually a very beautiful place in which to live and grow up as a child; the kind of town where everybody knew everybody and no one locked their doors at night.

I remember as a boy I would get up early in the morning, hop on my bicycle, and be gone all day. I had to be home at dark but besides that, I could go anywhere I wanted. Some days I would get up early, climb the mountain behind my grandmother's house, and play up in the woods all day long. I spent a lot of time alone as a child, but I liked it that way.

From the very beginning of my life, there was controversy. My mother was fifteen years old when she became pregnant with me. She was not married at the time, despite the myth that Appalachians get married when they are eleven or twelve years old. One thing that I can verify about the people in the Appalachian Mountains that is not a myth, they know how to keep a secret. It was an unwritten law that you told no one outside your family about anything that went on inside the family. Sounds like the Mafia, doesn't it? Maybe the Hillbilly Mafia would best describe it!

To this day, because of that unwritten law, I do not know the identity of my biological father. I found out later in life that there was some sort of secret that needed to be kept about his identity.

Anyway, everyone who knew the identity of my real father took that secret to the grave. I may have an entire family out there somewhere on my father's side that I have never met and probably never will meet. Oh well, unknown parents is also fast becoming a standard American way of life.

My family was somewhat dysfunctional depending on whose eyes you were looking through. Drinking and fighting was the norm, not the exception. I learned how to drink beer around the age of ten and I learned about fighting from before I can remember. I grew up in an environment that was somewhat prejudiced as well. I do not mean that we as whites disliked the blacks. I mean we disliked just about everybody! We did not discriminate our dislike against any one race or creed. When asked if I was a prejudiced person because of my upbringing my response was always, "Against who?" Where I come from, we disliked just about everyone! Red, yellow, black or white, we were prejudiced day or night! On the other hand, maybe it was just my family! Any way you look at it, the things I learned from my family would cause me troubles later in life.

As I stated earlier, my troubles started very early — actually, from the moment I was born. When I came into this world, I was not breathing and my heart had stopped beating. They tried for several minutes to revive me and just as they were about to give up, I screamed out. My mother always told me it was a miracle that I was alive but I did not agree with her. I have never really liked it here on Earth. I always thought, even as a little boy, that I did not belong here or that I came from somewhere else and one day I would go back home.

My mother tried to do the best she could raising me but because she was so young and because we were so poor, she had a hard enough time taking care of *herself.* I remember times when we had nothing to eat. My mother would take a slice of bread, spread butter and sugar on it, and bake it in a small oven. That would be our supper for the evening. We moved from place to place so I never really had a place to call home. One time we lived over the top of a liquor store and there was no heat. It was one of the coldest and miserable times I remember.

In what is fast becoming another standard American way of life, eventually my mother gave me to my grandmother. It happened very quickly too.

THE FAMILY DEPARTS

My mother had finally gotten married and they had two children together, which is how I ended up with two brothers and a stepfather. We were all living with my grandmother because my new stepfather did not have a job and we had nowhere else to go.

One Saturday morning, my grandmother sent me to the store and when I came back my mother, two brothers, and my stepfather were all gone. I asked my grandmother where they had gone and she told me my stepfather got a job in another state and they had moved. At first, I could not understand why they did not take me, but after my grandmother said she wanted me to stay with her, I did not think much about it anymore. After all, I guess I was the bastard out of the group and my stepfather took only his real sons. So just like that, my family was gone, but I was with the one I really loved.

THE LOVE OF MY LIFE

My grandmother! Now that is another story all by itself. Besides my two sons and my little brother, she is the only human being I have ever really loved. Along with being the most loving woman I have ever met, my grandmother could also be the meanest woman as well. Mean to everyone but me.

She was raised in a coal-mining town way back in what they call a "holler." For those of you who do not know what I am talking about, the word "holler" comes from the word "hollow." Hollow refers to a valley that is between two hills and it represents a "hollowed out space." In the Appalachian Mountains, this narrow passage or road is often used to reach a coal mine.

In those days, if you or a family member worked for the coal mines, the coal company owned everything. They owned your house, your clothes, and everything else you had. They paid the men who worked in the mines with what they called "script." The only place that you could spend the script was in their company store. If you complained, you were either sent out of the holler, if you were lucky, or you could just simply disappear.

My grandmother was married to one of those miners and together they had five children, two boys and three girls. One of those girls was my mother. One day her husband simply decided not to come home and left my grandmother to raise five children alone. She found out later he took another job in a nearby state and as far as I know, my grandmother never saw him again. He died of black lung, a disease common among coal miners.

After her husband left her, she was sent out of the holler by the coal company with nothing but her five children. That is one of the things I admired most about my grandmother — she was tough. Against all odds, she provided a home for her children. She did the best she could, considering her circumstances. I can tell you this; no one took advantage of her. She could fight like a man and did so on many occasions. She had her nose broken at least twice in barroom fights.

My grandmother liked her beer and she would take me to the bars with her. We had this little scam going. She would prop me up on a bar stool and all the drunks would come by and give me money. They would stumble up and say, "Here little buddy, take this money and buy yourself something." At the end of the night, my grandmother and I would split the take right down the middle. You would be surprised at how much money we would get some nights!

UNCLE JAMES

Everyone in my family was about half crazy. One night my Uncle James (her son and my mother's brother) came home with a gunshot wound to the shoulder. James was crying and my grandmother asked him what had happened. He said he was in this bar and for no reason the bar owner shot him. Yeah, right! My uncle was the biggest con man alive. His nickname was "Slick" if that says anything to you.

It turns out that the owner of the bar was an old man with Coke-bottle bottoms for glasses and my big strong uncle was picking on him. The old man got tired of it and shot him. When my grandmother heard this, she got so mad at my uncle for picking on an old man that she gave my uncle a good old-fashioned ass whipping, even though he was already suffering from a fresh gunshot wound. Man, I wish you could have seen this little old woman beating up my big strong uncle! She showed him no mercy! You see, my grandmother was always for the underdog. That is exactly where I got my strong feelings about that subject. I hate bullies and I will go above and beyond to destroy them if possible. She must have made some deal with the bar owner so no one would go to jail because every week she would send me to the bar and the owner who shot my uncle would give me five dollars. That may not sound like much in today's economy but to a poverty stricken little boy it was a fortune. That went on for years.

My uncle did not like me because he was jealous of my grandmother's love for me. Every chance he got he would mess with my mind. One night I woke up in the middle of the night and I felt something wrapped around my left leg. At first, I thought I had the sheet tangled around me. As I reached down to find out what it was, I felt something moving and as I moved, it started to tighten around my leg. The more I moved, the more it tightened. When I turned back the covers, I saw a big Blacksnake wrapped around my leg! Although paralyzed with fear, I managed to jump out of bed and run through the house screaming!

My grandmother ran out of her bedroom and tackled me. When she saw the snake wrapped around my leg, she almost left me to fend for myself. Blacksnakes are common in the mountains and can grow to be over six feet long. Thank God, they are not poisonous! They belong to the constrictor family, which is why every time I moved, it would tighten up. After about ten minutes, we managed to loosen the snake from my leg and my grandmother threw it out the backdoor. It took me weeks to get over that. I would wake up in the middle of the night screaming and my grandmother would come and stay with me until I fell back to sleep.

At this point in my life, I kept having the same nightmare repeatedly. I dreamed I had to walk along the edge of this giant razor blade. A thin layer of cotton covered the extremely sharp edge and every time I took a step, I was terrified that the blade was going to slice through my foot. It was rough going for a while, but I made it through with the help of my grandmother.

My grandmother and I could not figure out how the snake got into the house until one night my Uncle James came home drunk. While sitting with Gran (this was her nickname) and me at the kitchen table, he leaned over close to me and with this drunken smile said, "How did you like that present I put in your bed a few weeks ago?" Just then, a large ceramic plate came crashing down on his head! He fell to the floor unconscious and I looked up to see Gran standing over him. She looked straight at me and said, "I know he is my son, but I never did like that boy!"

From that point on, I made it my life's goal to do anything and everything I could to pay back my uncle. For example, he had several pairs of white shoes that he loved. I polished them all black in my spare time. One year he had gotten several hundred dollars' worth of fireworks right before new years, and he intended to sell them at a profit to all the neighbors. Unfortunately for him, I found them first. The neighbors did have plenty of fireworks to set off that New Years Eve, but it did not cost them a dime. I gave all of his fireworks away free of charge! I think if it were not for my grandmother, he would have killed me the first chance he got. He told me so on many occasions.

He tried to settle down later in life by getting married and having two sons. I am not sure if it took or not, because one time while he was still married, I caught him at Gran's house with another woman. He begged me not to tell and I said, "That will cost you fifty dollars." His face turned a nice shade of dark purple because he was so angry. However, he counted out fifty dollars and reluctantly handed it to me. I smiled and as I came down Gran's driveway, I met his wife driving up. She stopped and asked me if I had seen James and I politely replied, "I sure have. He is in Gran's house with another woman." It was amazing but her face turned the same nice shade of dark purple that Uncle James' had turned earlier. Imagine that! That was the best fifty dollars I ever made!

THE FAMILY RETURNS

My grandmother and I had a good daily routine going after my family moved to another state. She would get up every morning and leave for work at 6:00 a.m. She worked in a hospital laundry for over thirty years. Talk about hard work! She would stand there all day folding sheets, one right after another. No one ever gave my grandmother anything. She earned everything she had the honest way, with hard work.

I would get up at 6:30 a.m. and get myself off to school. I was in elementary school so this was a big feat, considering my age. I think it was probably around this time in my life that I started taking care of myself and not relying or needing anyone else. This too would cause me problems later in life. I had problems with communication in relationships because I was not willing to listen to anyone else. That happens after a while when you are used to being alone and making most of your own decisions. Anyway, I was very happy living with my grandmother.

One morning after she had gone to work, I heard a knock at the front door. I remember wondering why my grandmother would knock on her own door at 6:30 a.m. I opened the door to find my mother, my two brothers, and my stepfather standing on the front porch. Just like that, my family was back. They had been gone for two years, but it did not seem long enough for me. I did miss my little brother, Wayne, though. I loved him dearly. Before he left and especially after he got back, we were always together. Everywhere I went my little brother was sure to follow and I did not mind it one little bit.

TRAGEDY CHANGES A LITTLE BOY

Even though it may appear my childhood was not that great, I was a happy child until tragedy struck when I was twelve years old. Before I went into the sixth grade, I worked all winter to earn fifty dollars so I could go on a field trip with my sixth grade elementary class to our nation's capital, Washington, DC. I was so excited! It was the first time that I was going to be outside of our little town. We were set to leave on a Friday afternoon and return the following Sunday afternoon. Forty-eight hours, that was all I was going to be gone.

Ever since my family returned, I had become real close to my little brother, Wayne. Sometimes other children in the neighborhood would pick on him so I was constantly making sure that he was okay. After I put a few knots on some of their heads, they eventually left him alone. I loved him very much.

I had one final conversation with Wayne before I left on my trip. I specifically told him not to leave the yard. I especially told him not to cross the railroad tracks or the main highway. My grandmother's house was beside the railroad tracks and the long coal trains carrying coal from the coal mines were constantly racing through our little town. I was afraid one would hit him if he were to leave the yard and wander across the tracks.

That had already happened one summer. One afternoon I was delivering the evening newspaper and another kid from the neighborhood was helping me. He went down one street and I went down another. We planned to meet back at my grandmother's house for some cool lemonade and I beat him there. I was sitting on the porch when I saw my helper come up over this little hill onto the railroad tracks. Almost at the same time, we saw a freight train barreling down the tracks. The train was about 20 yards from him and he had plenty of time to take two steps forward to get out of the way of the speeding train. However, he did something that still baffles me to this day. Instead of stepping out of the way, he panicked and began running down the track trying to out-run the train. In no time at all the train swallowed him up and he disappeared.

The train engineer, seeing what happened, began to stop the train. Because it was very unusual for a train to stop in our town, people started gathering around when the train slowed to a stop.

I think I was in shock at what I had just seen because I remember just sitting there as people tried to figure out who had just been killed by this train. Maybe somehow I felt responsible since the little boy was helping me deliver papers when he was killed. I never told anyone what I had seen.

There were only bits and pieces of his body spread out along the tracks making it impossible to identify the victim. Finally the brother of the victim could not find his little brother and it was determined that it was he who was killed. I remember they were finding body parts for days and never really found them all. They spread lime over the area to keep the smell down. I felt so sorry for the victim's family, especially the older brother, but little did I know I would eventually find out exactly how he felt!

"Stay away from the tracks and the main road" was the last thing I said to my little brother before I boarded the big Greyhound bus for Washington, DC.

I had a wonderful time in our nation's capital. The thing I remember the most was visiting President John F. Kennedy's grave in

Arlington National Cemetery. He had recently been assassinated in Dallas, Texas. I remember they had a burning torch by his grave that was never to go out. The "Eternal Flame," they called it.

What a wonderful forty-eight hours, so I thought. On Sunday afternoon, I returned to my little hometown and as the bus pulled into the station, I wondered why I did not see my family waiting to greet my return. I was not overly concerned though considering they had moved away suddenly once before and left me behind. Maybe they had left again!

As I got off the bus, I saw my half-brother Rocky standing there with a strange look on his face. Rocky was my younger brother by one year. I asked him where everyone was and he said a car struck my brother Wayne that morning and he was in the hospital and not expected to live. It was at this moment that my heart felt like it stopped!

Apparently, Wayne had followed my mother, without her knowledge, out of the yard, across the railroad tracks to the main highway. A man who was returning home after a night of heavy drinking struck Wayne with his car. He was still drunk when he struck my brother and his car dragged his little body for two hundred feet down the hard asphalt. Wayne survived for eleven days in the hospital before succumbing to his injuries on May 19, 1964. Two little boys died that day, my brother Wayne and me. Wayne died physically and I died emotionally. I could actually feel my heart turn to stone and any hope of happiness slip away, only to be replaced by bitterness and anger. This was a marker in my life. This event started me on my downward path and it was not long before I was consumed by bitterness, anger, and hatred.

JUL • 64 •

This photo of Wayne was taken right before he died. It was finally developed two months after his death.

I remember the night Wayne died there was a lot of crying and screaming in the house. Everyone was asking why this had happened to such a sweet, innocent little boy. In the middle of the night, I heard someone on the back porch and I got up to investigate. It was my mother crying out to this thing called God. God was not something we talked about in our family except to take His name in vain. So, you can imagine my lack of understanding as to why my mother would be talking to Him.

I remember her words to this very day, some forty years later. She pleaded with God to let her die before any more of her children died. I remember thinking; *I hope she gets her wish!* You see, my heart had turned cold very quickly and already I was very angry and bitter, which only added to the misery caused by the loss of my brother. I did not realize it at the time but that very night I had become enemies with my own mother and this entity called God. In my mind, I blamed them both

14

for what happened to my little brother and I decided right then that eventually they were both somehow going to pay!

Although I was only twelve years old, I started my alcohol career about this time. It was not hard to get something to drink because everyone I knew drank. I would steal a few beers from Gran's refrigerator and she would never miss them. She also made corn mash liquor in her basement so I had access to all the liquor that I wanted. Do not get me wrong though, when I was caught drinking they would attempt to punish me, but after a while they just gave up. I would not do what they said so what were they going to do, kill me? I did not care one way or another!

The first time I can remember being drunk to the point of passing out was the summer between my sixth grade and seventh grade. That was right after Wayne's death. There was a group of winos that traveled around our town and I got to know them. Because I was under age, I would get them to go into the local liquor store and buy whiskey, vodka, or whatever I wanted. Because of my relationship with the town drunks, I became the man to go to if you were under age and wanted something to drink.

One afternoon I drank a pint of Popov Vodka all by my little lonesome and quickly found out that that was too much! Some concerned citizens called my mother and told them that I was lying in the parking lot of the local Dairy Queen unconscious. She freaked out and called the police (who happened to send my stepdad) because she probably thought I had been hit by a car. I can now understand her panic because it had not been that long since Wayne had been killed on that very same road.

Once everyone arrived and found out that I was only passed out drunk, they all had a good laugh, except for my mom. It was a long time before she forgot about that incident. I must have scared her to death.

From then on, I drank my way through junior high school and then high school. I have no idea how I graduated from either, because I never studied and skipped school most of the time to get drunk and party. I went all the way through school and never read one book from cover to cover. I remember the first book that I read in its entirety was a book called *The Exorcist*. I was in the Navy, on my ship in the middle of the ocean, with nothing to do, so I picked up that book and could not stop reading it until I finished it. Sad, huh? I often wonder if things would have been different in my life if the first book I had read had been the Bible.

I lost many friends in high school who died in alcohol-related accidents and I was in many car wrecks myself, but never got a scratch. I do not know how because most of the cars were totaled and most of the people with me were hurt, some very badly. At the time, I did not know or care why I was spared. Living or dying meant nothing to me. I do believe somebody had to be watching over me probably in hopes that I would eventually change for the better. You will be able to figure out who later in this book.

THE FINAL NAIL IN THE COFFIN

It appears God was listening to my mother's prayer that night on the back porch after Wayne's death, because she got her wish. Eight years later when I was twenty, she was murdered. She was shot behind her left ear with a .25 caliber pistol, in broad daylight while she was sitting in her car in the middle of downtown Charleston, West Virginia. The bullet exited her right eye. The man who shot her committed suicide and they found his body in someone's front yard early the next morning.

I was in the US Navy at the time. I remember routinely calling home to talk to my grandmother, as I had a habit of doing every week. When she answered the phone and realized it was me, she could not speak. Right away, I knew something was wrong and I knew someone else was dead. My aunt (my mom's sister) got on the phone and said, "Jackie, your mother is dead." I remember being stunned briefly, but only briefly. I asked what happened and she told me she was murdered. At the time, that was all they would tell me.

I was at a Navy friend and his wife's house when I made that fateful phone call. After I hung up the phone I remembering telling them that my mother had just been murdered. They were in shock but I was having a hard time gathering any emotions. Was I in shock or was I really that dead inside? I guess it was the latter because all I could think was how this murder was going to inconvenience me. I did not want to go back home. I did not want to be involved in another funeral. If my mother was dead then so be it! What did I care?

However, I finally decided to go home, but instead of thinking about how my return would show respect to my mother, I looked at it as an opportunity to party with my old friends.

The next morning the Red Cross contacted me and arranged for me to return home for my mother's funeral. Just like that, I was back in my hometown...a place I thought I had left behind for good.

I went straight to my grandmother's house. As I came down the driveway, there were cars parked everywhere. This was big news in my hometown. I am not positive, but I think she may have been the first person ever murdered there.

When I walked into my grandmother's house, she jumped up out of her favorite chair and hugged me as if she was never going to let me go. You see, by this time in my life, I was considered the strong one in the family. I was the one who went out into the world to make his fame and fortune. When I showed up, it was as if everyone was suddenly at peace. I always took care of things for everyone in times of tragedy. As I look back on it now, I was not strong; I was just dead inside.

Everyone in the family was at Gran's house that day, just sitting around like a bunch of zombies mourning my mother, and I was already thinking about sneaking away for a beer.

I asked my stepdad what had happened and he filled me in on all the details. As a police officer for our little town, he had all the inside scoop. Evidently, the individual who killed my mother had deep feelings for her and when she rejected him, he decided if he could not have her, no one would. Therefore, he killed her and took his own life shortly afterward. So many people for generations were affected that day all because of someone squeezing a metal trigger. For example, after my brother Wayne's death, my stepdad and my mother had had another child together. He was six years old at the time our mother was killed. He was almost too young to grasp the gravity of the loss of his mother. I remember him having a blank stare on his face throughout the entire ordeal. He was the only one for whom I truly felt some sort of sadness.

Next, my stepdad asked me something that really shocked me. He said, "Jack, we have to use the car your mother was murdered in for the funeral and it has to be cleaned first. Can you do it?" I asked why he could not do it and he said because there is still blood and tissue on the dashboard and he could not bear to clean it. I thought, *So, it is okay for the first-born child to clean his mother's brains off the dashboard of her car, but not all right for this big, tough police officer to do it! Sorry, I forget sometimes that I am the one who can do things like this and remain sane.*

Anyway, I ended up cleaning my mother's blood from the inside of the car because no one else was strong enough or perhaps, unlike me, they still had some sort of life and feelings left in their bodies.

It came time for me to see my mother for the first time since I had left home and joined the Navy. It was the funeral home policy to let the immediate family spend the first hour of the wake alone with the deceased. The rest of the family wanted to give Rocky and me some time alone with our mother, so we went in first. I still remember the funeral home smell, as my brother Rocky and I walked into the room together where my mother's body was lying in this big bronze casket. As I mentioned earlier, the flowers at a funeral have a unique smell that stays with you the rest of your life. It is a combination of flowers and death. I had encountered the same smell at Wayne's funeral.

The room had very little light and it was very quiet. As soon as we entered the room, I could see my mother's face just above the rim of the casket. When Rocky saw her, he immediately fainted and the funeral home personnel helped him outside for some fresh air.

I found myself all alone, walking up to my mother's casket. When I got close enough, I stopped and just stood there looking down on her lifeless body. You could tell that a bullet had exited from her right eye because they did not do a very good job of fixing it up for the funeral. It looked like they just glued her eyelid closed. I stared at her for a while, trying to gather some sort of emotions, but I could not. Instead, as I looked at her dead body I remember saying, "That's what you get!" and I turned and walked away. That is the last memory and image I have of my mother and it is not a very pleasant one. I do not remember much after that because I stayed drunk and high on drugs the rest of the time I spent in town before I returned to my ship in the Navy.

I think toward the end of her life my mother was trying to reach out to me but I did not make it easy on her. I was still angry with her for Wayne's death. For example, she wanted to come and visit me in Long Beach, California, where I was stationed in the Navy at the time. At first, I said no many times but I finally agreed and she arranged to come for Thanksgiving. Maybe this was to be the beginning of our healing process! Maybe I was going to finally restore my relationship with my mother! She never made it to California. She was murdered November 3, 1972, at the age of thirty-seven.

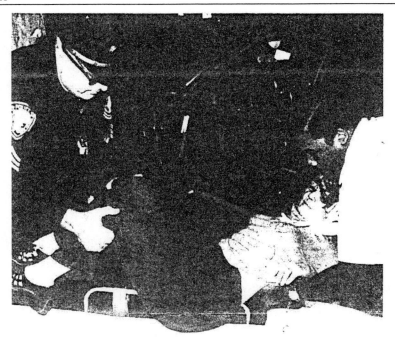

My mother after being shot

TO THE BOTTOM WE GO

After my mother's funeral, I returned to the Navy and continued my life of drugs, alcohol, women, and violence. My motto was, "The Navy … it's not just an adventure, it's a four-year drunk!"

I did anything I wanted, whenever I wanted. I lived a very self-centered, selfish life. I cared about no one, especially myself. You see, when you are dead inside it really does not matter if you live or die. I had no ambition or goals. I lived for today and today was mostly a nightmare. I have no idea how many times I came close to death. I was usually high on drugs or alcohol and even though I thought I was in control, I was totally out of control. That is the great delusion about drugs and alcohol. *You cannot look out from your life and see the truth, but people can look into your life and see the nightmare.*

20

I eventually ended up back in my hometown after I got out of the Navy, which was a big mistake! My drinking and drug activities escalated and soon I was even more out of control. My true friends stayed loyal to me, all three of them, but everyone else hated to see me coming. The only people that I half-way cared anything about were my grandmother and my stepbrother, who was born after Wayne's death. I certainly did not care about myself.

We were a heartless bunch and did many heartless things to other people. I remember one incident in particular. There was a guy who always wanted to drink and party with us but we did not like him because he had polio when he was a child and he walked with a limp. So one night after he passed out drunk, we took him to the local funeral home and put him in a casket. One of our drinking buddy's dad owned part of the funeral home so we had easy access to everything there. We dressed him all out and even put makeup on him.

We left him there and went on our merry way. Hours later, the police were called to the funeral home after someone reported screams coming from inside. Our victim had eventually become conscious only to find himself dead, so he thought. He was never the same mentally afterwards and for some reason he never wanted to party with us again!

Because I did not care about anything, death did not frighten me. Most people thought I was mean and were sometimes afraid of me but I did not see myself that way. There is a difference in people that qualifies them as being truly a mean person. I'll give you an example.

There was a kid who grew up in my town who was younger than my crowd and he used to get picked on a lot. Eventually he ended up serving time in prison. When he got out, he was all pumped up and a lot physically stronger than he used to be. No one picked on him anymore. One afternoon, we just happened to be in the same bar and I got into a fight with some guys. For some unknown reason, he started helping me with this fight. Probably because there were more than one guy trying to beat me up. We all ended up in the parking lot outside and after a little while, we won the fight. Both opponents were lying on the ground almost unconscious.

As we started to walk off, my friend stopped and returned to his victim who was still lying on the ground helpless at this point. He suddenly kicked the guy in the mouth, knocking all his front teeth out. As he turned back to me, I asked him why he had done that. We had already won the fight and there was no reason to hurt him anymore. He just smiled and said, "Why not!" To me, that is pure meanness. I never really set out to hurt anyone like that — it just happened sometimes.

Because of my lifestyle, I have had guns put in my face and have even been shot at a few times. I remember the only time I thought I was truly going to die was at the hands of a little old lady. I was at a redneck bar deep in the mountains with two of my friends. I could tell as we walked into the place that the locals did not want us there. It was the kind of place that if you had a full set of teeth, you were not welcome.

After a few hours of drinking, one of the locals approached our table and sat down uninvited. I could feel my body tighten up because I knew all hell was about to break loose. One of my friends had a habit of getting louder, the more beers he drank. By this time, he was shouting at everyone in the place, so I knew it was just a matter of time.

Our uninvited guest looked at my friend and said, "Why don't you just shut up!" Before he could answer, this intruder reached across the table and smacked my friend across the face, sending his glasses flying across the room. I was already in motion by that time, and I struck him in the jaw with my fist.

From that point on, things got a little blurry. The next thing I remember the person who started all this ran out the front door and I started chasing him. He ran around to the back of the bar and entered a screen door that lead into the kitchen. As I approached the door, a little old woman stepped in front of me. I was ready to crash through the door and roll over her, when I noticed she had something in her bony little hand pointed directly at my face. It was a .357 magnum pistol. I remember being shocked that this little old woman could even hold up such a big gun. She looked straight into my eyes and said, "That is my son you are chasing. If you take one more step, I am going to kill you!"

Now coming from the lifestyle that I did, being threatened that way was not that unusual, but this time was a little different. This time I knew that this person was about to pull the trigger. I could see it in her eyes. I thought to myself for a few seconds, and as I stared back into her eyes, I coldly said, "Go for it. If you don't, I'm going to bust this door down, break your scrawny neck, and then I'm going to kill your ugly ass son!"

Was I really that brave? No, I was really that stupid! I just did not care anymore. When you do not care, nothing matters, not even being shot in the face by a little old woman. As I prepared to die, to this day I do not know why she did not shoot. She took one-step back and closed the main door in my face. After standing there for a minute staring at the door, I quietly turned around, went back around to the front of the club and found my two friends lying in the parking lot. I looked at them and calmly said, "You guys about ready to go?" One of them said, "I believe so!" So, we loaded up and headed down the highway in search of another bar. We never spoke about this again and I never told anyone how close I came to dying because it would not have made any difference to them. This was our life and dying was eventually going to be part of it!

Also because of my lifestyle, I have been cut open and busted open. I wrecked every car I ever had and put many other people's lives in danger as well. I have spent time in so many different city and county jails I cannot remember them all. I was mostly locked up for fighting or being drunk. After a week or two, maybe sometimes longer, the police would let me go, provided I left their town. I did not care about going to jail because most of the time, I needed the rest or a place to stay and after all, I did not have anything better to do!

STEPFATHER'S DEPARTURE

As I continued my evil ways, conflict with my stepdad became an issue and one day we got into an argument about something, I do not even remember what about, but he told me he did not want me around my younger brother. As I look back on it now, he was right. I was a bad influence on him and I did not need to be around him. That bothered me a little bit, but only a little bit.

I had just gotten out of jail and I was living in an abandoned trailer in Cabin Creek, West Virginia, when I got word that my stepdad wanted to talk to me. I thought that was strange because we had not spoken in quite some time and, as far as I knew, he was still angry with me. However, one day after a previous night of heavy drinking, I decided I would go by his house to see what he wanted. I was really hoping to see my youngest brother.

I remember it was close to dusk as I knocked on the front door. It was a small house and the door was open so I could see him lying on his bed. Back in those days, most people did not shut their doors, much less lock them. I went into the house and said, "Hey, man. How are you doing? I heard you wanted to talk to me and I was in town so I thought I would stop by."

Just then, because I had been drinking the night before, nature called! I asked him if I could use his bathroom but I did not wait for an answer. When nature calls like that, you need to answer quickly!

After I was finished, I returned to his bed. I asked him if he felt like talking, but he did not answer. I was standing at the end of his bed and his eyes were looking at me so I did not think anything was wrong. I just thought he was very tired, so I told him I would come back another time, and walked out onto the front porch to leave.

For some unknown reason, as I started to step down onto the first step, I froze. Then it hit me! I had been there about fifteen minutes and he had not said one word to me! At first, I started to get mad and then I decided something was wrong. I walked back into the house and turned on the light. As soon as I saw him in the light, I realized he was dead. He had that look of death that I had seen many times before. His face was almost light blue in color and his eyes were half-open, staring off into space. I tried shaking him and calling out his name just in case, but deep down in my gut, I knew it was too late.

My mind started racing! My first thought was maybe they would think I killed him. I did not know what had happened to him at this point and I did not have the best reputation with people who had argued with me in the past. I quickly dismissed that thought and called the local police. There was no such thing as 911 in those days.

Soon the police and paramedics were there and they immediately said it looked like he had died of natural causes. It turned out that he had had a massive heart attack and died immediately, probably while I was sitting on the toilet, because he had just recently died. I thought to myself, *Man, what is it with me and dead people!* Then I thought it was probably better that I found him, not someone else. It would have been terrible if my little brother had found him. Then it hit me. *Oh my God, where is my little brother?*

Just about that time, I looked down the street and saw him coming. He was ten years old at the time and just four years earlier, our mother had been murdered. Here is this little ten-year-old boy coming home to find out his dad was now dead. I could not let him see his dad's dead body. I did not want him to have that image in his mind. Believe me, I have many of those memories in my mind and they last for a lifetime.

I grabbed my stepdad's car keys and went to stop my little brother before he entered the house. When I got to him I said, "Hey, buddy. Your dad is not feeling well and they are going to take him to the hospital so we need to leave now so we can meet him there." My logic at the time was to find some woman to break the news to him gently. I was too cold-hearted and I figured just blurting out that his father was dead to a ten-year-old boy somehow seemed cold.

I took him to our grandmother's house first. I told him to wait in the car while I talked to Gran. When I told her what happened she freaked! She started to scream and cry, so I had to leave.

Our next stop was to visit my stepdad's sister. I figured surely she would take my little brother aside and break the news to him gently. I was wrong! She did the same thing as Gran. So once again, I had to leave.

At this point, I was running out of options. I took him to the chief of police's house, thinking maybe his wife could break the news to him. Wrong again! I could not figure out why everyone was freaking out so much. Somebody needed to take care of this kid because I was definitely not capable of helping him.

Finally, I had no option but to tell him myself. It was just after dark so I took him to a place called Curry Holler to deliver the news. I left the headlights on, got out and walked around to the front of the car while he got out and met me there. I kneeled down, looked him straight in the eyes and said, "Hey, man, I got some bad news."

Before I could continue he said, "I know, it is about my dad. He is dead isn't he?"

I said, "Yes, he is dead." I will never forget what he said next. It haunts me to this very day.

He looked up at me with these sad eyes and said, "What am I going to do now? Who is going to take care of me? You cannot do it. You are a criminal."

Boom! Even with a dead heart, I knew I felt something at that moment. I looked at him and said, "You are right. I am not much but I will make this promise to you. I will make sure nothing ever happens to you and that you are protected and taken care of." He gave me a brief smile and then he gave me a big hug and started to cry. I do not know how long he cried but I let him hug me until he was finished.

That night I took my little brother back to his house and I stayed with him. I found myself sleeping in the same bed in which I had found his dad dead only a few hours earlier. I remember lying in his bed thinking what a mess we were in, but I was happy I had a place to stay for the night.

I kept my promise to my little brother. I took care of him and protected him in the years to come. In 1980, I moved to Dallas, Texas, and he moved in with our grandmother. I told him as soon as I was settled in and he graduated high school, I would send for him. Once again, I kept my promise. He lives in the Dallas-Fort Worth area to this very day. He has been in the same job for over twenty years. He has a beautiful wife and son and lives in a big house with a swimming pool in back. As I look back on it now, I realize that even in all of my evilness and wickedness, God used me to help a little ten-year-old boy in a time of real need. To God be the glory!

1980 — TO TEXAS AND BEYOND

How and why did I move to Texas? When I was in the Navy, I was stationed in Pearl Harbor Hawaii. While there I met a beautiful model and we began to date. Do not ask me what she saw in me because there was nothing there as far as I could see. When I was discharged, we lost track of each other until by some miracle she found me in West Virginia. She was living in Texas and came to visit me. Before she left, she told me, "If you do not get out of here you are going to die soon!" She asked me to visit her in Texas and after my visit, we both decided it was best for me to move there. So I packed up my bags and moved to the Lonestar State.

At first, not much changed when I moved to Texas. Alcohol and drugs still ruled and I was still doomed. It was not long before my new roommate threw me out because I was so wild, so I soon found myself on the streets of Dallas. I stayed on this path of destruction through the birth of two sons and two failed marriages. Do not get me wrong — I loved my sons but I just did not know how to show it. This is where my childhood environment and upbringing caused me problems. I never heard the word "love" when I was growing up. In fact, I was taught that telling someone you loved them was a sign of weakness. I never once heard my family tell me that they loved me or each other for that matter. I think my grandmother told me once but she was drunk at the time. Love was only a concept to me. One in which I did not understand. We were taught to use people for what we could get from them and then cast them aside. I became a master at destroying other people's lives and at the time, there was no love found in me!

Part II: HOW EVERYTHING CHANGED

That if you confess with your mouth, "Jesus is Lord," and believe in your heart that God raised him from the dead, you will be saved.

~ Romans 10:9 ~

Chapter 2

Transformation through Salvation

Do not conform any longer to the pattern of this world,
But be transformed by the renewing of your mind.
Then you will be able to test and approve what God's will is —
His good, pleasing and perfect will.
~ Romans 12:2 ~

There comes a time in everyone's life, whether you want to believe it or not, that God reaches out to you with an invitation to join Him. For those who accept this gift of salvation, they will be transformed from the things of this world and the Holy Spirit of God will renew their minds. My time had come with the birth of my first son. Thank God that He called my name!

THE PATH TO SALVATION

When my first son was born, something started to stir inside me. I knew I felt something but I could not figure out what it was. I did not know how to take care of him or even how to love him, so it was not long until the marriage crumbled and I found myself all alone working in Charlotte, North Carolina.

It was 1995 and my grandmother had died the year before. You can imagine how bitter and angry I was at the loss of the only true woman

I had ever loved. I got to see her before she died and the greatest honor that I've ever had was to be a pallbearer at her funeral. I got to carry my grandmother to her grave. For all those years that she carried me, I finally felt like I had a chance to pay her back just a little by carrying her to her grave. In case you have not heard this before, I loved my grandmother very much.

GOD WILL ANSWER YOU

Because I was now living and working in North Carolina, I was separated from my son who was twelve hundred miles away in Dallas, Texas. It did not take me long to figure out that without him I had absolutely no reason to live. As I look back on it now, that was my lowest point. I would start trouble everywhere I went because I did not care. One night I started a fight in a strip club that entertained mostly bikers. They beat up my friend and me and threw us in a ditch for dead. I thought it was funny but my friend stopped hanging out with me after that. I also remember driving down the interstate one night in the wrong direction on purpose. I was daring someone to hit me. I was so close to death but I did not care.

Then one Sunday after I had been drinking and smoking dope all weekend, I was sitting in my condominium that overlooked Lake Norman and I started thinking about my son in Dallas. All of a sudden, I was so sad because I could not be with him. I could not see his little face or give him a big hug. I became more and more depressed, but this time I could not blow off these feelings, as I had been able to do in the past. For the first time I was having difficulty drowning my feeling in drugs and alcohol.

Finally, I could not take it anymore and I realized it was either death or God. I decided death was out of the question so I talked to God for probably the first time in my life. There was a time in my life, when I was nine years old, that I went to church because my next-door neighbor talked me into it, but that didn't last long and I had no idea what it meant to be saved or to have a relationship with God. I think I was just going through the motions at that time to get a little attention.

Anyway, sitting on my couch overlooking Lake Norman with a joint of marijuana in my hand, I made a deal with God. I told Him that if He would somehow supernaturally get me back to Dallas so I could at least be in the same town as my son, I would walk into His house (meaning a church) and listen to what He had to say.

Now maybe, for most of you out there, that might not seem like a big deal, but for me it was. I was mad at God! I was at war with God! If you mentioned His name around me, there was going to be trouble. I spent all of my time doing things against God. He was the last person I wanted help from, but the pain of the separation from my son was too much to bear.

I finally passed out. I got up and went to work the next morning and I barely remembered my conversation with God and I did not think much about it. As I was walking down the hallway at work, I saw a guy I used to work with in Dallas. I walked up to him and said, "Hey, man! What in the world are you doing here?"

He said, "Hey, Jack! It is good to see you! The company I work for has just bought out the microfilm division here and I am here to announce it today."

I said, "Wow! It looks like we will be working together again." Then he lowered the boom! He said, "That's right, but after my meeting, I want to talk to you about going back to Dallas to take care of a new site we have there."

As he walked off headed to his meeting, I was paralyzed! I was literally paralyzed! I could not believe it! In addition, when I remembered my conversation with God the night before, I became even more paralyzed! Does God really answer prayer that fast? Does He really care about people who hate Him? Maybe He was striking while the iron was hot! Maybe He saw an opening in my heart and decided now was the time. I do not know what His motive was but just like that, within weeks, I was back in Dallas near my son.

I know what most of you are thinking: Did I keep my promise to God? Well, as soon as I got back to Dallas I headed to my favorite bar Graffiti's. The owner was a good friend of mine. After a few beers one night I said, "Hey Andy, I need to talk to you about something." He saw the seriousness on my face and came around the bar to sit beside me. I whispered, "Do you know where any churches are in Dallas?" He looked at me as if I was crazy.

He said, "What are you going to do, rob a church?"

I said, "Man, you know I am not a thief. I am a troublemaker. Let's keep things in perspective here!"

He then said that he had a girlfriend who went to a little church in Mesquite, Texas, called Galloway Avenue Baptist Church. He said, "If you are serious, then I'll go with you." I told him I was dead serious and that we would go this Sunday.

I kept my promise to God and found myself in church. The pastor there was a man by the name of Vic Bass. Everyone called him Bro Vic. For months I went to that church almost every Sunday, listening to that man preach his heart out, but with no results for me. I was hopelessly lost and it was starting to look like only God Almighty Himself would be able to reach me; and that is exactly what happened!

During those months, I had gotten married again and we were expecting our first child. I was also spending all the time I could with my first son, so life was good. I was still drinking and smoking dope almost daily while going to church every Sunday. I am sure I am not the only one who has ever done that and I bet there are many out there right now who raised holy hands on Sunday morning and lived like hell throughout the week, only to come back on Sunday to ask for forgiveness. What a vicious cycle!

DECISION TIME

It was at this time that I came to a crossroads in my life. On one side, God was calling me into His service and on the other side the world was calling me into sin. To make things worse, I was in the middle of a big drug deal that was going to make me rich. I knew some drug dealers on the east coast and I knew some I had been dealing with in Dallas. My plan was to create a pipeline from the southwest to the east and I would control it. Everything would go through me and the two parties would never even meet. That way I was the most valuable part of this deal and would remain somewhat protected for the time being.

The first deal was only days away from happening when God spoke to me. It was not an audible voice but He spoke to my spirit. Unless you have been there it is very hard to explain. He was reaching out His hand to me and He wanted me to join Him in the things He was doing.

What He said next finally got my attention. He said that this would be the last time He was reaching out to me and, if I did not join Him, He would have no choice but to leave me to the things of this world. I realized by that statement that He had been reaching out to me all of my life but I was too busy or angry to notice. That makes sense, because I should have been dead years ago. In the back of my mind, I always thought something or someone was watching over me, but I did not know for sure until now. All of those car wrecks with no injuries, the gun and knife attacks, the many fights that I survived, the gallons of alcohol I consumed, and the pounds of drugs I did, I should not have survived.

I was even struck by lightning one night when I was drunk. I remember it was raining hard and I was standing beside this house trying to stay dry when all I heard was a loud buzz. The next thing I knew I was ten feet or so away from the house face down in a puddle of water on the lawn. I have no idea how long my face was submerged in that water, but by rights I should have drowned or been killed by the lightening. I have cheated death so many times someone definitely had to be protecting me. Now I know that someone was God!

After God's message to me, my first thought was that it was not such a bad thing to be left to this world because I was getting ready to be very rich. I felt like I had been left to this world all of my life anyway.

BROTHER ROCKY DEPARTS

My second thought was that I had drunk so much alcohol and done so much dope that I had finally lost my mind. I kept thinking of my brother Rocky, who grew up normal and started having mental problems around the age of nineteen or twenty. He was eventually diagnosed as a paranoid schizophrenic and struggled with that disease until he died in 2001.

He died a horrible death. In the middle of August, he sat down on the edge of his bed to take his pants off and according to the coroner had a mild stroke. The stroke did not kill him but it left him incapacitated. He could not get up from his bed to call for help and had forgotten to turn on the air conditioner in the apartment. For five days, he laid there in the August heat until he finally succumbed of heat exhaustion. He literally dissolved into the mattress and floor. Some neighbors finally noticed the smell and alerted the local police. I was notified and flew to West Virginia to make his funeral arrangements.

When I got there, I went to the funeral home to make arrangements and they told me there was a problem. Because Rocky's body was so badly decomposed, dental records were going to have to be used to make a positive identification. The law stipulates that the body has to be positively identified before it can be buried. The problem was that the dentist was not going to be available until Monday afternoon and the funeral was already set for Monday morning. Because I have always been the one to make the tough decisions, I told the funeral home director that we would go ahead with the funeral without the body inside and when he got Rocky's body released he could take it to the cemetery and put it in his casket. It was going to be a closed casket anyway. I was also going to be the preacher who presided over the funeral so I would take care of everything. I was already a Christian when Rocky died and on my way to becoming a preacher, which is how I ended up preaching his funeral.

And so it was. I preached my brother's funeral and prayed at his graveside with no body in the casket. Later that afternoon, the funeral director called me to tell me Rocky's body was in his casket and he was officially buried.

Anyway, back to my path to salvation. Rocky had mental problems most of his life and I thought the same thing was happening to me at this big crossroads in my life!

MY FINAL DAYS TO SALVATION

It was a Sunday morning when God spoke to me. It was not an audible voice like the one we use to communicate, but rather it was as if he was speaking directly into my spirit. Do not ask me how I knew it was God because I cannot explain it. I knew exactly who it was and I understand exactly what He was saying. I think only a person who has an encounter with God like this one can fully understand. His message was clear and simple. "I need you to come with Me" is all He said.

I did not think much about it most of the day but then it started. On Sunday night, I started crying! Can you believe it! I do not think I cried when I was born. I think I just looked around and said, "What's up?" Not only was I crying but also every terrible thing that I had ever done was passing before my eyes. It was as if a movie of my life was playing in my mind and I could not stop it.

In addition, all these different kinds of emotions were flooding my body; emotions that I had never experienced before. It was terrible and the only thing I could think of to escape this torture was to get high and get drunk, which was exactly what I did.

I got wasted Sunday night and when I woke up Monday morning the crying and emotions started all over again. I remember going to work and having to slip into the restroom throughout the day to cry and wash my face so no one would realize what I was doing. I got wasted Monday, Tuesday, and Wednesday nights and each morning it started all over again. I cried more during those four days than I had cried my whole life up to that point and I had no idea why I was crying!

Finally, Thursday rolled around and I could take it no longer. I had to have help and I did not know where to turn. I had no friends who would understand what was happening. They would all think I was just high or drunk. Then I thought of Bro Vic at Galloway Avenue Baptist Church. Maybe he could help me through this nightmare. However, there was a slight problem with Bro Vic and me. He had done something I did not like some months ago and I called him up and cussed him out one night. I am not talking about a few little cuss words but it was an old-fashioned cussing-out. I also threatened his life, so I was pretty sure he was not going to help me. However, I kept getting an overwhelming feeling to call Bro Vic so guess what I had to do! That's right — I had to eat the biggest crow-sandwich ever and call him. *Talk about humbling yourself!*

It took me forever to dial his number and I was praying he would not answer so I could leave him a message and not have to face him. However, we all know God does not work that way.

I think Bro Vic answered the phone *before* the first ring. I said, "Hey, Bro Vic. You know who this is?" If he replied no, then I thought I could still hang up and back out of this nightmare.

He said, "Jack Williams." I said, "That's right. I am sorry to bother you but I need help." Now here is what real Christians act like. It would have been very easy for him to say, "I cannot help you based on our last conversation." After all, I had threatened to kill him! He boldly said, "How can I help you?" I asked, "Can you meet me in the church? God is calling out to me and right now the only place I feel safe is in the church." He said, "How fast can you get there." I said, "I am on my way."

It was Thursday night, June 19, 1996, at 6:25 p.m. when I entered Galloway Avenue Baptist Church. No one except Bro Vic was there when I entered the sanctuary. This was a true man of God because for all he knew I was luring him there to hurt him or possibly even kill him.

I told him what had been going on and he said it sounds like I needed to accept Jesus Christ as my Lord and Savior. For the first time in my life, I agreed and the war began! Bro Vic then said, "Let me know when you are ready," and he started praying from the front row of the sanctuary.

While Bro Vic was praying, I started pacing back and forth fighting something, what, I did not know exactly. I eventually started walking around the inside of the sanctuary along the outer wall. This lasted a few hours until as I passed by the cross in the middle of the sanctuary one more time and I got physically sick. Finally, I looked up from my hands and knees and said to Bro Vic, "I am ready."

He immediately got up, came to me, and we prayed together for God to forgive me of my sins. I confessed to God Almighty that I was a sinner and I asked Jesus Christ to come into my life to be my Lord and Savior.

Then, as God is my witness, I could actually feel things leaving my body! When those things were all gone, I suddenly felt as though this giant burden lifted from me. I felt free and at peace for the first time in my life!

Do you know what my first thought was after I was saved and as I looked to the cross? I said aloud, "Now I can see my brother Wayne again someday!"

Glory, hallelujah! I was finally saved and nothing could ever change that. What a wonderful feeling of security!

STARTING THE CHRISTIAN LIFE

Being saved was a wonderful thing but after I left the church that Thursday night, I still had to face the same world. Although I was now a Christian, there were still things going on in my life that did not line up with God. Remember, I had this big drug deal getting ready to happen. *How was I going to get out of this?* After all, I was the one setting it up. I was the key player! I thought about it and the only thing to do was to go face them and tell them the truth. I had a bag full of weed that they gave me to keep me happy until the deal happened, so I gathered it up and went to see them. My wife at the time had no idea what I was getting ready to do. I never told her a thing about it because I thought she would be safer that way.

I went to the small apartment in North Dallas where my drug business partners and I used to meet and I knocked on the door. They opened the door and I walked in with the bag of dope. There were four Mexican men in the room waiting to greet me. I recognized two of them but did not know the other two. *This was a big red flag!* Even if I had not been a Christian, I would have killed the deal at that point because I had a strict rule about bringing unknown people to a meeting.

At first, they were happy to see me and then they saw the bag. I told them that the deal was not going to happen because I was now saved and God would not approve of this. They looked at me as if I were crazy! One of them actually said, "You are crazy! You are the deal! Without you, there is no deal! It is too late for you to back out now!" At this point, I started to think I was not going to walk out of this little apartment alive.

I remember asking myself, *did God allow me to be saved right before I was going to be killed?*

I looked at them and said, "The deal is not going to happen. I am out. Here is your dope. I am going to turn and walk out of here and we will never see each other again. I am sorry." I suspected that they all had guns and I did not have one with me. As I turned to leave, I really did not have any fear though. If they were going to kill me, I could not do anything about it anyway. I felt as though each step I took brought me closer to God. As I closed the apartment door behind me, I felt relief because now my drug world was over and I could be free to serve God.

Here is a slight insight as to God's mercy. Right after that, on the Fourth of July weekend, bounty hunters from another state arrested their leader and took him back to face some pre-existing charges. Local Dallas police arrested everyone else and I would have been arrested with them if I had been there. The deal was doomed from the beginning, but I did not know it. I believe that God saved me just in time. For some reason that I did not know at the time, God decided to show me mercy. I love that song lyric, "He's an On-Time God. Oh yes He is!"

I talked to their leader briefly some months later while he was still in jail. He said he was tired and really wanted to change. I told him about God and maybe it was time for him to give up this worldly life and start living a Godly one. He said he was really thinking about it and I believed him. I have never heard from him since nor do I know what happened to him. I would like to think he is part of the Kingdom of God today!

MY FINAL CRIMINAL ACT

On top of all that, even though I was now saved, I also still had some criminal charges for which I would soon have to go to trial. I committed those crimes before I was saved, but I still had to suffer the consequences of my actions, Christian or not. Remember, my second wife

41

was pregnant with my second son (my first with her) and it was beginning to look like I was going to spend the birth of his life in jail. I arranged for my brother and my friend Andy (the bar owner) to help my wife through the delivery and bring the baby home. I was not sure how we were going to survive as a family with me in jail.

The day came when I had to go to trial. I said good-bye to my wife as she dropped me off in front if the Lew Sterrett Justice Center in downtown Dallas, Texas. I did not want her there in the courtroom watching as they handcuffed me and took me off to prison. I was sure that I would get at least two years behind bars.

I remember sitting with my lawyer as the trial began and staring at the door that led to the jail from the courtroom. I was thinking that soon I would walk through that door into a nightmare. However, I was prepared to face reality and the consequences of my sins.

I thought about praying to God to get me out of this now that I was a Christian, but I felt like I would be putting Him on the spot and that did not seem right at the time. After all, He had already saved me from the Mexicans, the Dallas police and granted me an eternal place in His Kingdom so I figured he had given me a lot more than I deserved.

As the trial was going along, things did not appear to be going my way. I was guilty and it seemed like everyone knew it and I was just waiting for the judge to drop the guilty verdict gavel on me.

Then it came time for the arresting officer to testify. As I watched the police officer walk to the stand, something seemed wrong. *Then it hit me.* This police officer was not the arresting officer. When I was arrested, there were seven police cars involved in the chase. However, there was only one police officer who actually saw me commit the crimes that initiated the chase, and this police officer taking the witness stand was not him. The prosecuting attorney had made a big mistake.

I leaned over to my attorney and whispered, "This guy was not the arresting officer. Does that make a difference?" My lawyer's eyes got as big as saucers and he said, "Are you sure?" "Without a doubt," I replied.

After the prosecutor finished questioning him, it was time for my lawyer to cross-examine. He asked only two questions. He looked at the witness and simply asked, "Sir, were you the arresting officer and did you see Mr. Williams commit the crimes for which he stands accused today?"

The police officer looked stunned and replied, "No."

The judge almost had a heart attack! He looked at the police officer and said, "You mean you were not the arresting officer? You mean you cannot testify that the defendant committed the offenses for which he is accused?" The officer meekly replied, "No Sir."

The judge looked at me, gave a dirty look to the prosecuting attorney, slammed his gavel down and shouted, "Not guilty. This case is dismissed!"

My lawyer looked at me and said, "What did he say?" I replied, "He said case dismissed. Let's get out of here man!" And just like that, I walked out of Lew Sterrett County Courthouse a free man. My lawyer told me that in all his years of practice he had never seen anyone set free like he had just witnessed. He said God must have shown me mercy. I then realized that he was exactly right. God not only showed me mercy, but He had my wife and soon-to-be-born son in mind as well. What an awesome God we serve. I was guilty and yet He showed me mercy, not justice. Amen!

However, the story does not end there. Since that day in court, I do not think I have burped in the wrong direction! Needless to say, I have not been arrested since then. My wife went on to give birth to my son and we were serving in the church where Bro Vic was the pastor and where I was saved. Life was good!

43

One Sunday morning, as Bro Vic was preaching, about midway through his sermon, somewhere from the back of the sanctuary someone shouted, "I need to be saved right now!" Just then, I saw the back of this man's head walking past us down the aisle toward the pastor. As he passed, I noticed something familiar about him. When he got to the front, he turned around and boom! There in front of me was the police officer who tried to testify against me at my last trial! *I told my wife and she almost fainted.*

There are over 2000 churches in the Dallas/Ft. Worth metroplex. What are the odds that police officer and I would end up in the same church! Now here is how God works. That police officer went on to give his life to Christ and we ended up becoming good friends, serving God in the same church. Only God can take two men from opposite sides of the law, and bring them together to serve Him. Amen!

SERVING OUR KING

For the past eighteen years, my love for Jesus has never ceased. I have not had one drop of alcohol or smoked one joint since the night I surrendered to God. I have not committed adultery, got into one fight, or been locked up in jail. Only God can do something like this! I did not have the strength or the desire to change myself — but God did! He saved me and He can do the same for you. I do not care how bad you think you have been. God can and will forgive you, and you can be adopted into the family of God!

Eventually I became an associate pastor at Faith Family Church in Diboll, Texas, where Bro Vic is the pastor. By this time, my oldest son from a previous marriage had come to live with Brandon and me, making my life complete.

However, just when you think things are perfect just the way they are, here comes God; and to my surprise, He called me out of the church. It was the same scenario as before eighteen years earlier when He called me to salvation. I was happy with my life the way it was and had no desire to change it. However, I was obedient to His call and resigned from the church.

At first, I did not know what He had in mind. I thought maybe another church or something along those lines. I had no idea what God was about to use me for but I was in for the surprise of my life.

Given my background and the many tragedies, where is the last place on earth God would send me to witness to the lost? If the answer is surprising to you one can only imagine how floored I was when He revealed His will to me. God in His infinite wisdom wanted me to go to death row in the State of Texas to minister to convicted murderers! I am going to be honest; I had several problems with my new assignment. After all two people in my life were murdered. In addition, I spent most of my life trying to staying out of jail. Now the creator of the universe wants me to go into a prison surrounded by convicted murderers and tell them about Him! My immediate answer was a definite no. So how was God able to change my mind?

In 2006, God blessed me with a great job in Houston, Texas. It truly was a blessing because being a single dad means I pay for everything. Do not get me wrong; taking care of my sons has been the greatest blessing I have encountered so far in this world, after my salvation. I have been raising my second-born son by myself since he was two years old. He recently turned nineteen.

I eventually had to move to Houston so I could be closer to my new job. However, this presented a problem because I still wanted to keep attending my church, which was now one hundred miles away in Diboll, Texas.

Every Sunday morning, my sons and I would get up at 5:00 a.m. and make the one-hundred-mile drive to Faith Family Church. I had to be there at 8:00 a.m. to practice the music for the day because I was the music minister. Then, after the service, we made the one-hundred-mile drive back to Houston. We usually got home around 2:30 p.m. We did that for twenty-eight months until finally God revealed that is was time for my sons and me to leave for good. I was probably supposed to leave twenty-eight months ago but like many of us we try to hold on to the past things we are comfortable with instead of listening to God and stepping out in faith in His timing, not ours.

So finally, I resigned from Faith Family Church as the music minister and associate pastor and started visiting churches in the Houston area. I received the shock of my life during this time. I thought I was just going to walk into a church and everyone would come running up to me with open arms. I was very disappointed. Some churches ignored me and others made me feel like an intruder. I could not believe it. During this time, I realized how far off base most churches have become. Most have become social clubs and if you do not meet a certain criteria, you are not welcome. I am positive this is not what God had in mind. Anybody should be able to walk into any church at any given time and feel the love of God upon him or her. I am sad to report that is not the case. You can argue with me if you want but try it sometime and see what you find, especially if you are single. It was apparent to me that most of the churches I visited are structured towards families. However, I finally realized that I was in very good company. I remembered a guy who lived around two thousand years ago who was single and the church rejected Him also. His name was Jesus Christ! *I feel better!*

Eventually I ended up visiting at Grace Church in Humble, Texas. I love their music and the pastors. However, I have been going there for over five years and no one there even knows I exist. It is a large church with one service on Saturday night and three on Sunday morning, so you can see how easy it would be to stay anonymous there. I go every

Wednesday and Saturday nights. I normally walk in, speak to the ushers and find a seat without speaking to anyone else.

Do not get me wrong. Grace Church is a wonderful church with wonderful pastors and people. I have not made any effort to get involved so I take responsibility for part of my anonymity. However, there is something wrong when a person, especially a preacher, can attend services faithfully every Wednesday and Saturday nights for over five years and no one knows who you are. That is one of the dangers when a church gets too big.

However, one Saturday night as I was finding my seat, out of the corner of my eye I saw this large man staring at me. For some unknown reason, I stopped and turned toward him. He immediately extended his hand and following my preacher instincts, my hand automatically came up. He introduced himself and we talked briefly and found out we knew some of the same people at Faith Family Church in Diboll. His wife is good friends with the wife of one of the praise team members that I led. Small world ... *or was it?*

On another Saturday night, he told me just in passing that he ministered to inmates on death row in Livingston, Texas. I remember my first response was something like, "Wow! You will never catch me in there. I spent most of my pre-Christian life trying to stay out of jail!" He just laughed and encouraged me to pray about joining him. I told him I would pray about it but I had no intention of going into the biggest maximum-security prison in Texas to minister to murderers on death row. I wanted to ask him if he was crazy but I restrained myself.

However, if you are a Christian, you know how God works sometimes. He puts circumstances in your path to speak to you about His will for you. If you have not already learned, the very thing that you say you will never do when it comes to serving God, is more than likely the very thing you will end up doing. The rule-of-thumb is this: if God puts something on your heart and you cannot forget about it, you might as well get ready to do it.

Anyway, one thing led to another and I finally listened to God and went through training from the Texas Department of Criminal Justice. I was now ready for my first visit to death row.

How can I walk into death row and share the Gospel of Jesus Christ with murderers just like the one who killed my brother Wayne and my mother? For one thing, as a Christian, you do not get to choose your assignments. If God tells you to do something, you need to do it whether you understand it or not. In fact, it is better that you do not understand, because if we can understand it, then we have a tendency to rely on our own understanding instead of having faith in God to guide our every step.

In addition, if I call myself a Christian, how could I not do His bidding? I am not that same heartless man who stood beside his mother's casket many decades before. I am a new creature in Jesus Christ. I have turned from my evil ways to the goodness of Jesus Christ. God Almighty Himself has softened my heart, and He has prepared me for this ministry on death row in the state of Texas. So here we go!

PART III: WELCOME TO DEATH ROW

Whoever sheds the blood of man,

By man shall his blood be shed;

For in the image of God

Has God made man.

~ Genesis 9:6 ~

Murder is defined by Wikipedia as the unlawful killing, with malice aforethought, of another human, and generally, this state of mind distinguishes murder from other forms of unlawful death (http://en.wikipedia.org/wiki/Murder).

Have you ever thought about how a person can become so overwhelmed with evil, causing them to commit this horrible act against a fellow human being? It seems like, after Adam sinned against God, all hell broke loose and ever since, we humans have been going downhill fast. How did we get to the point where a person hurts another, even until murder, especially when God commands us not to murder?

I think deep down inside we know we are doing wrong yet we do it anyway. The Apostle Paul, who was inspired by God to write most of the New Testament in the Bible, said, *"I do not understand what I do. For what I want to do I do not do, but what I hate I do* (Romans 7:15). Even Paul struggled with understanding why we do the things we do. I often wonder how Judas, one of Jesus's disciples, even after he spent so much

49

time with Jesus, was able to betray Him, knowing Jesus would suffer horribly before He was eventually executed. Although he did not nail Him to the cross, he murdered Jesus just the same. All sin is horrible, but in my opinion, murder is at the top of the list.

MURDER IS BORN

It did not take long after man fell into sin for the first murder to occur. Adam and Eve, the first man and woman created by God, had two sons named Cain and Abel. Portrayed as sinful, Cain committed the first murder by killing his brother Abel. He was mad because God rejected his offerings but accepted Abel's. Why did God do that?

Genesis 4:3–5 gives us some clues. It says that Abel *"brought fat portions from some of the firstborn."* He offered some of what came first, as opposed to waiting until an animal had plenty of offspring (and the oldest were reproducing themselves) and then sacrificing one of the youngest. Abel also offered the choicest parts. He was clearly giving the best of what he had to God.

Cain, on the other hand, brought *"some of the fruits of the soil,"* which were not necessarily the best crops — they may have been damaged or what Cain considered extra or leftover. Abel's and Cain's actions were a reflection of their attitudes toward God — should God receive the best of what they had or not? — and it was their attitudes that God was concerned with. Thus Cain was the first human born (remember Adam and Eve were created not born) and the first murderer, and Abel was the first victim of murder.

I often wonder what was going through Cain's mind when he murdered his brother. Surely, he knew that he would suffer the consequences of his actions or was he even thinking about the consequences? Cain and Abel had grown up together, so I assume there had to be at least some brotherly love between them. It appears Cain was consumed by the *evil of jealousy*. In our judicial terms today, Cain committed first degree, premeditated murder. He thought about it, planned it, and carried out his plan. He could not plead that he killed in a moment of anger when he was temporarily insane. He could not say that there was a fight. In plain fact, he assassinated his brother. Therefore, it would appear that Cain somehow got to the point where his focus was on himself and not God, which allowed the evil of jealousy to consume him.

Another great man of God from the Bible was Moses, whom God chose to lead the Israel Nation out of bondage from the Egyptians. During this undertaking, he was able, only by the power of God, to perform many miracles, including the parting of the Red Sea. Even though he was a great man of God, he was also a murderer. Moses murdered an Egyptian slave master and fled into the desert. What was Moses thinking when he murdered this Egyptian slave master?

At this point in Moses life, he did not have a relationship with God. He murdered *out of ignorance*, because of his lack of knowledge of God. Does ignorance mean that Moses was evil or mean? No, ignorance means a lacking of knowledge or information on a particular subject or fact. Moses was knowledgeable of man's law and ignorant of God's. Does this justify his actions? No, we are still held accountable by both.

King David from the Bible was described by God as a man after God's own heart (Acts 13:22). What a wonderful thing to have God say about you! However, David, who started out as a shepherd boy, who slew Goliath and later went on to become king of Israel, eventually became a murderer because of *his lust for a woman*.

David committed adultery with Bathsheba, the wife of Uriah the Hittite. Bathsheba became pregnant. David sent for Uriah, who was with the Israelite army at the siege of Rabbah, so that Uriah may lie with his wife and conceal the identity of the child's father. Uriah refuses to do so while his companions are in the field of battle and David sends him back to Joab, the commander, with a message instructing him to abandon Uriah on the battlefield, "that he may be struck down, and die." David marries Bathsheba and she bears his child, but the Bible says, "but the thing that David had done displeased the Lord."

David received three punishments from God for this sin. First, that the *"sword shall never depart from your house"* (2 Samuel 12:10) second, that *"Before your very eyes I will take your wives and give them to one who is close to you, and he will sleep with your wives in broad daylight. You did it in secret, but I will do this thing in broad daylight before all Israel"* (2 Samuel 12:12) and finally, that *"the son born to you will die."* (2 Samuel 12:14). Even though David repents, God struck the child ill and *"On the seventh day the child died."*(2 Samuel 12:18).

In our eyes, David's punishment might seem as harsh as our death penalty today. However, debating the validity of the death penalty is not the purpose of this book. I personally cannot decide on the death penalty one way or another. I know what the Bible says about it and I know what man says. However, God has not called me to get into the middle of that debate.

I am not there on death row to convert them to my beliefs, but rather to present the Gospel of Jesus Christ to them and let the Holy Spirit of God convict them of what they need to do. I tell them up front that I cannot save them — only the Holy Spirit of God can do that. However, if they want, I will be more than happy to tell them how to be saved according to the Word of God. I do not force my beliefs on them. I have watched other chaplains try that and most of the time they end up pushing the inmates away. The choice has to be theirs and theirs alone.

Also by interacting with these convicted murderers, I might gain some insight as to the big question, "Why?" Join me now as we enter one of the most violent and most depressing places on God's Earth!

Chapter 3

The Prison Ministry Begins

Some sat in darkness, in utter darkness,
prisoners suffering in iron chains,
because they rebelled against God's commands
and despised the plans of the Most High.
So he subjected them to bitter labor;
they stumbled, and there was no one to help.
Then they cried to the LORD in their trouble,
and he saved them from their distress.
He brought them out of darkness, the utter darkness,
and broke away their chains.
Let them give thanks to the LORD for his unfailing love
and his wonderful deeds for mankind,
for he breaks down gates of bronze
and cuts through bars of iron.
~ Psalm 107:10–16 ~

FACTS ABOUT TEXAS DEATH ROW

In 1999, the Texas Department of Criminal Justice (TDCJ) moved death row from the Ellis Unit in Huntsville, Texas, to the Polunsky Unit in Livingston, Texas. The Polunsky Unit houses over three hundred death-row offenders as well as around two thousand other offenders for various offenses. Death-row inmates are located in a separate building from the other inmates and are housed in single-person cells measuring sixty square feet (6' × 10'), with each cell having a very narrow window. Death-row offenders also have recreation individually. Offenders on death row receive a regular diet and have access to reading, writing, and legal materials. Depending upon their custody level, some death-row offenders are allowed to have a radio. The women on death row are housed at the Mountain View Unit.

How does an inmate end up on death row? Not all people who murder someone end up on death row. Believe it or not, Texas has certain guidelines that define a capital offense, for which if convicted, you will receive the death penalty.

Texas Capital Offenses

The following crimes are capital murder in Texas:

- Murder of a public safety officer or firefighter;
- Murder during the commission of kidnapping, burglary, robbery, aggravated sexual assault, arson, or obstruction or retaliation;
- Murder for remuneration;
- Murder during prison escape;
- Murder of a correctional employee;
- Murder by a state prison inmate who is serving a life sentence for any of five offenses (murder, capital murder, aggravated kidnapping, aggravated sexual assault, or aggravated robbery);
- Multiple murders; and
- Murder of an individual under six years of age.

In addition, Texas has another law on the books that can render you the death penalty whether you actually pull the trigger or not. It is called the "Law of Parties."

Law of Parties

Section 7.02 of the Texas Penal Code outlines the following: A person is criminally responsible for an offense committed by the conduct of another if "acting with intent to promote or assist the commission of the offense he solicits, encourages, directs, aids or attempts to aid the other persons to commit the offense" or "If, in the attempt to carry out a conspiracy to commit one felony, another felony is committed by one of the conspirators, all conspirators are guilty of the felony actually committed, though having no intent to commit it, if the offense was committed in furtherance of the unlawful purpose and was one that should have been anticipated as a result of the carrying out of the conspiracy."

What this essentially says is that you can be guilty of murder by association and you do not have to actually be at the crime scene. Case in point: a man hires another person to murder his wife and the plan is carried out. All parties involved receive the death penalty.

TIME TO GO TO JAIL

For you Christians out there, this next part is for you. Have you ever had a conversation with God and you were essentially dictating to Him what was going to happen? Let me explain. I think I have mentioned that I was not keen on entering this prison. On the ride up from Houston to Livingston, which is a fifty-mile drive, I was giving God some guidelines once I set foot inside the prison. I know, sad! I told God that I would know the moment I set my foot inside the front door of the prison whether it was Him who sent me there or whether it was man's idea. How did God answer? He did not say anything as I arrived at the prison.

On December 7, 2010, I entered the Polunsky Unit Prison in Livingston for the first time. My purpose was to minister and spread the Gospel of Jesus Christ to any inmate on death row who would listen.

There are no words that can describe this place. You have to experience it to actually believe that places like this exist. No television show or movie can capture the reality of this place.

As I drove up to the prison for the first time, I had mixed emotions. At first glance, it was impressive. It sits out in the middle of a big field surrounded by barbed wired fences. As you turn into the prison, you first drive down this straight road for a quarter mile to the first guard shack. The guard asks you what you are there for and sometimes searches your vehicle. When he is satisfied, you then move forward to the parking lot situated in the front of the main entrance.

Fencing surrounding the prison

As I got out of my vehicle to enter the prison, I noticed large guard towers at each corner of the prison. I could see the silhouette of an armed guard in each tower watching every move I made.

Guard tower

Main entrance to the prison

When I walked across the parking lot and as I stepped into the main building that houses the check-in station, I immediately got my answer from God. As my foot touched down inside the prison for the first time, I had immediate peace. It was almost as if I had been there before and they were waiting on me to come back! It is hard to explain but I knew that this was where God wanted me to be at this exact moment in my life. Thank You, Lord Jesus!

The first thing that hit me was the smell. It smelled like a combination of mold, disinfectant, perspiration, and bad food. Parts were old and needed painting. All of the guards stopped what they were doing and immediately looked at me. One of them said, "Can I help you?"

I answered, "Yes. I am a volunteer chaplain and this is my first time inside." They smiled and proceeded to instruct me on what I needed to do to get through their security process.

The first thing you have to do is remove everything from your pockets and put your possessions into a plastic basket so they can go through a metal detector, just like at the airport. The only items you can bring into the prison are a pen, glasses, car keys, and your driver's license. Your belt and shoes need to go through the metal detector as well and then a guard motions for you to walk through another metal detector (just like at the airport).

After I went through the metal detector, the guard instructed me to face forward and stretch my arms straight out. Standing behind me, he began to search me by patting down my body. He was looking for any kind of illegal contraband I might be trying to smuggle into the prison. After he searched my body, the guard instructed me to raise each foot so he could see the bottoms of my feet; I guess so you cannot smuggle something into the prison taped to the bottoms of your feet.

After he says you are clean, you collect all of your belongings and check in with another guard. This guard verifies that you are on the authorized chaplain's list. If so, they take your driver's license and issue you a volunteer's badge. You get your license back when you leave the prison.

The guard opens the door and you walk across an open area through the razor wire fences that lead to what the prison calls One Building, which houses all administrative functions for the prison. From the first door you enter to the last door before you approach an inmate's cell door on death row, you pass through eighteen prison doors. You are about as deep inside the prison as you can get. You are not walking out of there unless they let you walk out! There is a sign on one of the doors inside the prison that says, "NO HOSTAGES BEYOND THIS POINT", which means, if I am taken hostage, I am on my own. They will not let any inmate out. I do not remember that mentioned in the training but it is too late now. I am inside!

Death Row 12 Building

Death row is in what the prison calls 12 Building. In order to get to the row you are escorted through the general population side of the prison. They call it "catching a ride." You literally have to walk through inmates who are free to roam in certain areas. I am not very fond of that but I believe that God sent me here so I also believe God will protect me.

General population

While waiting for a "ride" (escort) to death row, I had to wait in a small room near the prison chapel and inside that room was an inmate sitting quietly. He was a "trustee." These inmates have more privileges because of their good behavior or their trustworthiness.

I took this opportunity to speak to the inmate and strike up a conversation. After a few pleasantries, the inmate expressed his excitement at the possibility of being paroled next year. I asked him how long he had been there and he said twenty-five years. I hope he did not notice but I felt like my jaw dropped to the floor! I found myself face-to-face with a man who had been in that prison for over half of his life because he stated that he was forty-five years old. I started to ask him if he was sure he really wanted out because the world outside of these prison walls can be very difficult as well, but I kept my comments to myself. The reality of this place was starting to creep in.

After about five minutes, my guards arrived and I was escorted to 12 Building which houses nothing but death row inmates. As I entered what is referred to as the "row", I was amazed at the amount of steel bars everywhere. Long corridors with a steel gate about every thirty feet lead to areas divided into pods.

Gates from pod to pod on death row

These pods are lettered A through F. Each pod has two levels or tiers, with cells side by side all the way around the pod, and they are sectioned off into sections labeled A through F.

Pod with two tiers

The cells are steel boxes measuring 6' × 10'. They are equipped with a steel bed, steel sink, and a steel toilet.

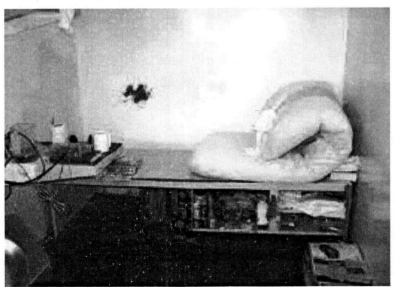

Death-row cell

Each cell has a solid steel door and on each side of the door is an eight-inch wide window running from the top of the door to about halfway. Each window is covered by steel wire, which allows only a person's fingertips to pass through. These small windows are the only way to talk to the inmates.

Inmates are locked in their cells twenty-three hours a day, seven days a week, three hundred sixty-five days a year. They only get out for approved visits by the media or family members, or one hour per day in what is called a "day room" for recreation, or to take a shower. I cannot imagine that type of isolation or captivity.

Cell doors on death row

In order to talk to the inmates, I had to wear a protective vest and be constantly escorted by a prison guard. I would soon find out that getting and keeping a prison-guard escort was going to be my biggest obstacle in this place.

PRESENTING THE GOSPEL

I had no idea how I was going to interact with these men but I had a feeling that no two of them were going to be alike. Therefore, my plan was to listen and learn.

At first, I imagined my biggest challenge in presenting the Gospel was going to be bringing Jesus into the conversation. I planned to look around their cell for anything that would suggest something about Jesus, perhaps a cross or a Bible. Once we were talking about Jesus, then my primary objective would be to present the Gospel of Jesus Christ to them and it would probably be different each time. I have memorized the Romans Road, which is a common method used in witnessing to a lost person. I have also broken it down into two *whys*, one *what*, one *how*, and one *who*.

Once I feel comfortable enough with an inmate (or anyone for that matter), I ask them if they are saved. If they answer yes, then I ask them to tell me about their salvation experience. The most common answer I receive is, "Well, I was baptized when I was twelve." To which I reply, "Wow, that is great! Now tell me about when you were saved." Baptism does not mean salvation. At this point, I have their attention, so I proceed down the Romans Road.

I start by explaining the first *why* in understanding why we need to be saved. I believe one of the most alarming facts facing the church today is the number of people sitting in church every week thinking they are saved but, in reality, they are lost. This happens because they do not understand what it means to be saved.

In Romans 3:23 God says, *"For all have sinned and fall short of the Glory of God."* In this verse, God has established that regardless of how good we think we are, we are still sinners in the eyes of God. Whether we believe this or not does not change the fact that it is true.

The second *why* is defined in Romans 6:23, *For the wages of sin is death, but the gift from God is eternal life in Christ Jesus our Lord.* In this verse, God tells us the consequences of our sins. Because we are sinners, we will suffer death. This death is not a physical death. Everyone is going to experience a physical death. No one gets out of here alive!

64

God is referring to a spiritual death. A spiritual death resulting in separation from God for eternity.

At this point, God has a problem. Have you ever asked yourself why God created you? The answer can be summed up in one word: Love. What good is it to have love if you have nothing or no one to express it to. Because God's love is so great, He created us to share it with Him. If we will just accept His love, He has so many wonderful things to give us. However, because God is holy in nature, He cannot be a part of any kind of sin, so at this point, because we are all sinners, we were all doomed to be separated from Him forever.

So *what* did God do about this? Romans 5:8 says, *"But God demonstrates His own love for us in this: While we were still sinners, Christ died for us."* These are amazing words! God sent His Son Jesus Christ to die for us not because we were good enough but because He loved us enough. Now because of this sacrifice, if you choose, you can be reunited with God through the shed blood of His Son!

How can you be reunited with God? Romans 10:9 says, *"That if you confess with your mouth, Jesus is Lord, and believe in your heart that God raised Him from the dead, you will be saved."* This is how you become a Christian. The word "confess" here means to agree with. Therefore, you must first agree with God that Jesus is His son, and then you must believe in your heart that God raised Jesus from the dead. If you do these two things, God says you will be saved.

Finally, just in case you think salvation is not offered to you because of the things you have done in your past or are currently involved in, God tells us *who* can be saved. Romans 10:13 says, *"For everyone who calls on the name of the Lord will be saved."* That means you!

The final and most important part in accepting God's gift of salvation is to pray and ask God into your life. Here is an example of what to pray when inviting Christ into your life:

Dear God, I know I have sinned and that my sins separate me from You. I am sorry for my sins. I believe your son Jesus died on the cross for me so my sins can be forgiven. I believe Jesus rose from the dead and is alive today. God, please forgive me. I repent of my sins and ask you to come into my life and be my Lord and Savior. I will obey You and live for You the rest of my life. Thank You. Amen.

So there you have it. This is how you can lead someone to God or if you have doubt, how you can make sure of your own salvation.

Finally, it was time to visit with my first inmate! As I approached my first death row inmate, you can imagine I had a full gambit of emotions. I had no idea what to expect. Were the inmates going to be friendly or was I getting ready to meet some mean and crazy people?

Chapter 4

Today I Die At 6:00 P.M.

Nebuchadnezzar then approached the opening of the blazing furnace and shouted, "Shadrach, Meshach and Abednego, servants of the Most High God, come out! Come here!" So Shadrach, Meshach and Abednego came out of the fire, and the satraps, prefects, governors and royal advisers crowded around them. They saw that the fire had not harmed their bodies, nor was a hair of their heads singed; their robes were not scorched, and there was no smell of fire on them.

~ Daniel 3:26–27 ~

Before we meet our first inmate, I want to share a near-death experience from another inmate who was scheduled to die, went to Huntsville State Penitentiary to be executed, and received a stay of execution at the last minute. Instead of being executed at 6:00 p.m. that evening, he was loaded back into a van and sent back to death row. Here are parts of an email he sent to family and friends. If you can, try to imagine yourself in his position and prepare yourself for an emotional rollercoaster ride! This is what happens from an inmate's perspective in his own words the day before and on the day of his execution.

THE CONDEMNED MAN SPEAKS

Ever since I learned I had an execution date set for October 18, 2012, I have been telling everyone that I very much planned on still being here on October 19, 2012, and here we are! God is good! I am alive and well and still in God's loving hands. I wanted to write this letter for a number of reasons. I want you to know what yesterday was like for me. All that I went through, the ways in which satan intensified his attacks on me, the way in which God countered that attack, and what it was like when I got the news that I was not going to die that day.

The past three months of my life have been extremely tiring and trying for me. I cannot explain to you how hard I have fought this fight. I can tell you the devil was inside that cell constantly tormenting me and the only thing that kept me from giving up was the vision God had given me earlier concerning my situation. The vision told me to keep fighting the fight and never give up and that God will continually strengthen me in my weakness. I am aware that I am a strong individual, but there is no way I would have been able to endure these last few months without God's strength.

People like to say that God walks with them, but I know that I stopped having the ability to a walk alone a long time ago! God has been carrying me these past few months and I thank Him. I understood that the battle I was fighting was not so much against the state of Texas as it was a spiritual battle. I now completely understand why God had to give me that vision a few months back. That vision was the key to me being alive today. I had to keep going back to that vision over and over again. See, a good rule of thumb when you are not getting new revelation from God is to go back to the last word that He gave you and remember it. I did not need a new word — I needed to continue to put the word He had already given me into action and that word was not to cross that line of disbelief and to choose life.

I had to keep choosing life over death on a daily basis in order to get to the victory. That is why I was so single-minded. There was no room for doubting. God gave me a word, and I obeyed His command and I had no doubt that He would show up. There was no thought of what if He didn't show up. All I focused on was life and getting that date off my back.

On October 17, the day before my execution, I had a media visit after my visit with my parents. So I did not get back to my cell until around 3:00 p.m. I did a few things, then I laid down to take a nap, thinking that I'd likely be up late that night because my initial plan was to try to type a couple of letters. When I woke up it was second shift and I spoke to the officer, explained to her my situation and asked her if she would try to pull my mail out so I would not have to be up all night waiting on it. In the meantime, I started packing up all my property knowing that as soon as I left my cell the next morning for my execution, they would come, look through everything, and then take it out.

As I was packing, this song kept playing inside my head. It was the Sam Cooke song, "A Change Is Gonna Come." I really like that song but not on this night and I will tell you why. In Spike Lee's movie *Malcolm X*, there is a scene at the end of the movie right before Malcolm X (played by Denzel Washington) is murdered. There is this close-up shot of Malcolm as he is walking down the street, headed for the Audubon (where he is murdered) and that song is playing in the background.

Well, along with this song playing inside my head, I had this image of that scene from the movie and this feeling of oppression just started overwhelming me. It was never a conscious thought on my part, but I am sure that somewhere in my head was the idea that this is my last night and that I am packing these things for the last time.

I tried to give no space to such a thought or idea but that feeling of oppression would not leave and I simply could not shake it. I went to the shower, I prayed while in there, and the feeling still would not go away. I asked God to please get that feeling off my back, but it remained. It was almost as if a physical presence was pressing down on me, trying to take me over; it felt like the specter of death was riding my back. I had no idea what it meant, but I knew that I did not like it and I know I was walking around that cell with a very confused look upon my face.

A little later, the officer came to my door and brought me my mail. Most of my stuff was packed and I was just leaving a few things out that I had planned to put up after I dealt with the mail. With the way I was feeling, I did not even really feel like reading my mail. Since mail call is the highlight of my day most days, maybe you can get some idea how bad I must have been feeling. I got eighteen letters that night and I was thinking, "I don't even feel like reading all this crap!"

I decided to read my mail anyway and as I am reading it, I still did not feel well. I was getting to the point of physical discomfort. One of my friends sent me some messages from some of the people who were out there praying for me. Normally that would have made me feel great. However, that night it had no effect. The other mail as well was just not enjoyable because of the feeling of oppression that was on me.

Then I came across a letter from my ex-wife, and at first I was thinking, "It took you that long to write me back and at a time like this?" I haven't heard from her in months and now that I have an execution date, I finally hear from her?

I decided to read her letter anyway and she explained to me that law school had been extra demanding lately and she simply did not have time to reply to the last letter I had written. She decided to write now even though she thought she would probably say something stupid at a time like this. This is what she considered stupid:

It's crazy because I am excited to see how God shows up. It's really a countdown at this point ... I'm sure you've probably had some

70

spiritual experiences these last couple of days and probably will continue to have them until Thursday. I am definitely thinking of you and praying for God to really come through and really show up. I am expecting something big ... I will respond to your letter (Thursday or Friday). How's that for faith ... can't wait to see you ... You know more than anyone that God's got you.

At a time when barely anyone is acting normal and I can sense behind all the smiles almost everyone is still so filled with fear of the "what if", this was exactly what I needed to read! As I was reading this rather short letter, that feeling of oppression completely left me. Whatever it was could stay there no longer and I went on with my night feeling joyful. That was a very timely word that I believe God used to reaffirm once again what was to come. I was now exhausted so I decided to try to get some sleep because I knew tomorrow was going to be long day!

EXECUTION DAY

I woke up early Thursday (my execution day) and got ready. The officers came by and asked if I wanted an early shower. I told them that I did want a shower but that I wanted to wait until I came back from the execution chamber until I took it. The female guard looked at me kinda crazy, then told me that she hoped I did come back.

Shortly thereafter, I was going to visitation. When I get out there, my two best friends are supposed to be out there, but they are nowhere to be found. So after I spoke with my spiritual advisor for a few minutes before she left for her other visits, I just sat there waiting. In the quiet of that visiting booth, satan set in on me like a hungry lion attacking a lame antelope! Negative thoughts started coming at a rapid pace. I did not meditate on any of them, but I heard them and they were not nice thoughts. I won't even dignify them by writing them out but just know that he was very much in that room with me. So much that I had to verbally rebuke him!

About that time, I saw two of my close friends coming in. I spoke to one for a few minutes. She told me that because of a bad wreck on the highway they were late. But that, in the midst of all that, she saw what she believed was a sign to her from God. As they were driving, a vehicle in front of them had a bumper sticker that said "Anthony." On another vehicle beside that one, was another bumper sticker that said "God Saves." She put those two together and felt a little more confident about the day. We prayed and she left to let my other friend come in.

Now let me show you how the devil works. I rebuked him from coming at me directly so he used my second friend to try to continue his mission to implant doubt in my mind. He used her fear and doubt to try to get to me. She says, "I know you are not going to like this and you might get mad but I am going to say it anyway." I am thinking she is going to start telling me what she thinks will be her last good-byes but she does something very unexpected. She tells me that if the execution goes through today, there will be some kind of service and … that is where she lost me! I told her on a day when I needed all my strength, I was not going to entertain that kind of conversation. So she left and then my dad came in.

We were visiting and talking about various things. We ended up just telling stories about friends and girls and other stuff that men talk about. At some point, I had him walk off so I could pee in my bottle and when he got up an attorney gave him a card for me. This was a card that some fellow inmates back on death row had all signed for me. It was a good-bye present. As my dad is reading it to me, an officer comes in and tells us that the warden is watching in the camera and he saw the guy hand my dad something. Of course, my dad gave the officer the card and he took it away. I said goodbye to my dad and next it was time for a minister friend to come in and once again, God showed His faithfulness because this man had a word for me from God that was *exactly* what I needed to hear.

He told me something that made me think that he must have been inside my head. He told me that right now the devil is trying to do everything in his power to try to make me give up. No matter how good I have been running the race of faith, it is the finish that is most critical, and I needed to finish strong. He told me to refuse to listen to any of the devil's lies because if he could get me to believe him instead of God that I would be giving him legal authority to take this away from me. He told me that faith comes by hearing but by hearing the wrong things we can build up negative faith. He reminded me of some spiritual principles that in that moment I really needed to hear. He spoke directly to my needs. We then prayed and finally it was time for me to gird my loins and get ready to enter into the most critical and most strenuous part of this fight — and to finish strong.

My time of visitation was up so they pulled me out of the visiting booth and got me ready to walk down the walkway back to death row. Two brothers were on each side with me. One of them, God has used numerous times to bless me with a word. He was there once again encouraging me to finish the race and to hold on. As I walked down the walkway, I heard my fellow inmates beating on the windows in support.

Next, I go into the death row building and walk to the back of the building, where I stripped, put on new clothes and went through all the motions of being chained up. Then I walked outside to a waiting van and we started the forty-mile ride to Huntsville. I had not eaten anything for 7 ½ days when I got into that van and I had not consumed anything outside of water for nearly two days. Good thing, too, because I got carsick with the way they were driving. Remember, I had not been in a vehicle in over 12 ½ years!

We get to the Walls Unit at Huntsville State Prison and this is where everything changes. All these years, I go everywhere in handcuffs but a few hours before they think they are going kill me, they want to treat me like a man. No handcuffs.! They talked to me with total respect and even shook my hand!

They took off all the restraints, gave me a pair of starched pants and a button up shirt. They fingerprint me, then put me in a cell. There was a big plate of all kinds of cookies and pies and cupcakes. I am not big on sweets but I ended up breaking my fast with three oatmeal raisin cookies. My plan anyway was to break my fast over there so I did it with my favorite cookies.

My next plan was to talk on the phone to everyone I could get in touch with, but first the chaplains had to explain to me about the procedure and how they do the execution. Both chaplains knew where I stood as far my faith because we had talked a number of times while I was on death watch, but they still had to do their jobs. I did not pay them any mind.

After that, my plan was to allow a few of my friends from out of the country to call me from 2:00 to 3:00, then to call some people locally from 4:00 to 5:00. Since I found out that a few people were not going to call, I used the first few minutes to make a call to my mom then to some other relatives and friends. All were short because I was waiting on my other friends to call. Things kind of got messed up so I only ended up talking to two out of the three. However, those mistakes had nothing to do with me. The warden's secretary messed up my overseas phone calls.

At least I got the two that I got and I was able to fulfill my word to a friend from Austin as well. I was also able to thank my mom. I was in high spirits and confident with expectations, thanks to the word God gave my minister for me. I did not allow any contrary thoughts to enter into my mind. I was perfectly at peace, smiling, and joyful.

At this point they moved me into a different place before 3:00 p.m. so I could talk to my spiritual advisor, Kathryn Cox. I was testifying to Ms. Cox and we were really having a great time of fellowship, when I noticed they started bringing in the real food. It looked good and smelled good! All kinds of stuff too! You have to remember, for years I have been eating trash. I was preparing myself to eat everything I could, as fast as I could.

All of a sudden, at about 3:25, the phone rings and it is my attorney. They asked if I wanted to talk to him and, of course, I accepted the call! At this point, I did not think he would have any news because I have heard that any information on a stay of execution comes closer to execution time. Man was I wrong!

He told me that the Supreme Court had granted me a stay of execution and that they had ruled 7 to 2 in my favor! I immediately started doing three things! Praising God, thanking Jesus, and crying. I could hardly talk at this point. I have some very emotional friends and all of them were crying either out of joy, relief, or just because. I myself was altering between smiling, laughing, and crying.

They have a rule that if you get a stay before 4:00 p.m. you do not get to eat any of the special food they had brought already. As they took the food away, I was not very upset though. They could have it! I'll take a stay of execution any time over their so-called special last meal. I say screw that food!

At this point the TDC media came back to ask me if I had a statement. They had already asked me if I had any final statements but I declined because to give a final statement meant I was expecting to die instead of living; and I was expecting to live all along. I said sure and began telling them all about all God. More or less I told them that God had given me a word telling me that I was not going to die on death row and that every step of the way He has proven faithful. He gave me

75

everything I needed to stay focused on the prize, He had spared my life, and He deserves all the glory!

And just like that, it was time to return to death row at the Polunsky Unit in Livingston, Texas. They gave me my death-row jumper back and put all the restraints back on me and we got back into the van. The driver commented that the drive back would seem a lot shorter than the drive over there. There is justice sometimes. Just like on the way over to Huntsville and the death chamber, I got motion sickness and threw up all over the van. They will remember me for sure!

When I got back to death row, I never thought I'd be so happy to see this hell hole again but considering I was still alive, it was good to see the old place. It might surprise you but many of the guards expressed their happiness about me coming back. They put me in a new cell and here I am once again locked up on death row, but very much happy to be among the living!

What did I learn from this experience? I learned that God is very faithful. I feel that through this experience I had to walk through the fire in order to get to where he wanted me to be in my relationship with Him. He allowed me to actually enter the lion's den and to walk into the fiery furnace. However, he also closed the mouths of the lions and brought me out of that fire without my clothes even smelling like smoke! Yesterday, I was literally ten steps from death's door and God brought me back. I knew I had to walk through the fire, but it was not to destroy me but to purify me. It has definitely worked because in these last few months I have come to a new place of purity and what I have gone through has birthed in me a stronger desire to serve God even more.

I pray that I never have to walk through this fire again. I pray that I never have to go over to the death chamber again. However, to know that I have been and come back is an experience that I do not regret because it has increased my trust in Him! I knew before that He had me. Now I know for sure that He has me! To God be the glory!

BROJACK'S FINAL COMMENTS:

I know that this is just a glimpse of the experience an inmate goes through when they are about to be executed and receive a stay of execution only to live another day. However, we will never know the experience of an inmate who is actually strapped to a table and his veins filled with poison until he is dead. We are about to meet some men who went through that very experience.

Chapter 5

A New Creature in Christ

Therefore, if anyone is in Christ, he is a new creation; the old has gone,
the new has come!
~ 2 Corinthians 5:17 ~

Michael Hall, Inmate # 999346

According to the Bible, Christians are brand-new people on the inside. The Holy Spirit gives them new life, and they are not the same anymore. We are not reformed, rehabilitated, or reeducated — we are recreated. At conversion, we are not merely turning over a new leaf; we are beginning a new life under a new master.

Strapped to a table in the death chamber at Huntsville Prison in Texas, moments before he was to be executed, Michael Hall claimed that Christ had changed him. I personally believe that God can change a person into a new creature in Christ but it has to be that person's decision. Here are my interactions with Michael on death row in Texas weeks before he was executed. Since Michael is among my first encounters, I am asking myself several questions at this point. Am I going to be able to stand face-to-face with a man who I know has killed another human being? Am I going to have compassion for him knowing firsthand the devastation murder causes? Was I really going to be able to tell him about Jesus without a judgmental heart? What was this murderer going to be like? I prayed, *God help me as I start this journey.*

CRIME CONVICTION: On February 15, 1998, Hall and one codefendant abducted a nineteen-year-old white female from a public street and drove her to a remote location. Hall and the codefendant shot the victim several times with a pellet pistol and several times with a .22 caliber pistol causing her death. They were caught at the border when they were attempting to leave the state and enter into Mexico.

DECEMBER 7, 2010

Today I met death-row inmate Michael Hall for the first time and he has an execution date of February 15, 2011. I did not know who to talk to first so I just went to the first cell to the left on the bottom tier. My plan was to move from left to right and hit all the lower cells, and then I would move upstairs and do the same.

As I approached Michael's cell door, I quickly became very cautious because at first glance he was a scary looking guy! At 6'2" and weighing around 230 pounds, when he approaches you, it can be a little intimidating. I really was not concentrating on why he committed his crime at this point — rather I was concentrating on surviving this encounter!

Immediately I had a problem. I had already heard from the prison chaplain and the warden that even though these inmates are locked in their cell that can still hurt you. The can make spears as hard as steel by peeling the paint from their cell walls. They keep rolling it until it becomes very hard and sharp. If you get too close, they can stab you. In addition, they can throw bodily fluids on you in hopes of humiliating you. Therefore, I immediately set a rule for myself. If I could not see both of their hands, I would keep a safe distance from their cell door. *I might be crazy but I am not stupid!*

Michael was dressed only in his white boxer shorts and as he approached his cell door, it felt like he was a giant towering over me. As I mentioned earlier, one of the things I struggle with in this place is the smell. Sometimes the inmates are not the best at hygiene, many times through no fault of their own, so their body odors alone are sometimes hard to endure. You add the smell of the old building, the food, and the fact that someone may have just finished using the restroom in the cell next door; to their own body odors and you sometimes have some overwhelming odors to endure. I mainly have to deal with bad breath. Because the row is so noisy and some of the inmates are soft spoken, you have to get very close to the inmate's door sometimes just to hear them speak. This is both dangerous and unpleasant. The TV shows and documentaries you see cannot capture the different smells in this place. It is something you have to experience to understand.

I was expecting this big husky voice from Michael but instead I was face to face with a gentle giant. He spoke in a very soft voice. I introduced myself as a volunteer chaplain and asked if he felt like talking today. I decided I would always respect their time even though I knew they had all the spare time they needed, that is until they are executed. I quickly learned it is all about respect in prison. In addition, when I ask if they feel like talking, it gives them the opportunity to decline if they do not want to talk.

To my delight, he agreed to talk with me. He told me his name and began talking about a book he was reading. I decided to just mostly listen and use this first-time encounter as a learning experience on how to interact with the inmates.

However, it quickly became apparent that I would not be able to keep my mouth shut. I could feel the desire to talk about Jesus welling up in my spirit. I was looking for an opportunity to bring Jesus into the conversation when to my surprise he started talking about his relationship to God. That was my cue!

I eventually found myself asking Michael if I could ask him a question. He agreed and I asked, "If you were standing before God today at the gates of heaven and He asked you why He should let you into His kingdom, what would you say?"

He thought about for a minute and said, "Because I belong to your Son, Jesus Christ."

I replied, "Good answer!" When I ask anyone that question, I am looking for a response in one form or another that they have put their faith in Jesus Christ, therefore opening up the gates of heaven to all of those who believe in Him. We talked about God and compared some scriptures and I was really feeling good about this first visit.

Michael then started talking about his execution date coming up but he did not seem overly concerned. That can mean one of two things, either he is confident in his relationship with God or he does not understand the consequences of dying without accepting God's gift of salvation.

Finally, I suggested he read Revelation chapters 21 and 22 because these chapters give us a brief glimpse of heaven. I was hoping it would give him some comfort to read about the place where he would soon be going. My plan was to pray for him all week and come back next week and talk to him further concerning his salvation. Just to make sure.

Even though he was at first glance a very scary-looking guy, Michael was actually a very pleasant person to talk to. I looked forward to my next visit with him and I learned very quickly not to judge someone by the way they look.

DECEMBER 21, 2010

The next time I got another chance to visit with Michael was two weeks later. I was starting to find out that many people on the row really want to talk to someone besides the guards, so I am quickly becoming very busy. As I approached his cell, he seemed in good spirits, but one never knows a person's true feelings. He started talking about another book he had just received and seemed very excited that he had finally gotten it. To us on the outside, it does not seem like a big deal to have access to a book, but to a death-row inmate that is very important. Those books are their only means of escape from the reality of their situation.

Suddenly I had to leave with the guards while they returned a pair of handcuffs to the control booth. The policy is that all handcuffs have to be accounted for at all times and this guard had forgotten to turn his in. I am beginning to find out that you never know how much time you are going to have with an inmate, so each minute is precious. Anything can happen on death row at any time, causing you to lose your escort or be asked to leave. Today, my visit with Michael was cut short but I hope for more opportunities to talk with him in future visits. Keep in mind; I do not just visit one inmate when I go to death row. I average about ten to fifteen per visit.

DECEMBER 28, 2010

I had a little trouble getting into the prison today. That sounds a little weird. Some people have trouble staying out of prison, not trying to get in! The guard could not find the list provided by the resident chaplain with my name on it, allowing me access. I thought I might have made the fifty-mile trip for nothing but praise God there was still a state chaplain there to get me inside the prison. I met him in One Building, which is the administration building, and he and two guards escorted me to death row. It was about 3:00 p.m. and some of the pods were already getting their dinner when I arrived on the row.

I decided to visit Michael first since his execution date was fast approaching. As I mentioned earlier, you never know when you are going to lose your escort and your visit will be cut short. Under those conditions, I did not want to take the chance of missing an opportunity to talk with Michael.

Once again, he seemed to be in good spirits despite his circumstances. I asked him how he was doing and he gave the generic answer "fine." After some light conversation, I could not take it any longer! I asked, "Michael do you mind telling me about when you got saved?" Even though I was almost sure Michael was saved, I wanted do my best to make certain. If the state of Texas had their way, Michael did not have much time left on this Earth.

Michael replied, "Because I have put my faith in Jesus Christ and accepted God's gift of salvation, I am now saved." Good answer! That was exactly what I was looking for. I felt better about the salvation of Michael Hall. I found myself at that very moment thanking the Lord for the opportunity to meet Michael and for allowing me to spread the Gospel.

Now that I felt comfortable about Michael's salvation, I found myself trying to imagine why he committed such a horrible crime. Did he understand what he was doing? Was he just an evil, violent person? Based on his demeanor and our conversations, he did not match the crime he was convicted of committing. Maybe I will get an answer and maybe I will not. That is not my purpose and I am fine with not knowing that part.

FEBRUARY 1, 2011

I have not been to death row for a few weeks because they were on lockdown. During a lockdown, no visitation is allowed and the inmates are not allowed to leave their cells for any reason. The guards search each cell for contraband such as cash, alcoholic beverages, cigarettes, lighters, any controlled substance, cell phones, weapons, unauthorized correspondence, illegal drugs, etc. During this period, the inmates are served only sandwiches and Kool-Aid. It is not an enjoyable experience for anyone involved. It is a lot of extra work for the guards and a rough time for the inmates. However, there is no other way to completely control unauthorized contraband so these lockdown periods are necessary and can last several weeks.

VOLUNTEER BANQUET

Before I talk to you about my next visit with Michael, I want to tell you about a banquet I attended during the lockdown period. On January 18, 2011, the Texas Department of Criminal Justice held a banquet in Livingston for the local volunteer chaplains in the Polunsky Unit Prison. I was very impressed. They had barbequed brisket, which was very good. They had several speakers at the event and among them was Warden Tim Simmons of the Polunsky Unit. He gave a very good speech about how vital volunteer chaplains are to the morale of the prison. This made me feel good to know that the prison administration was behind what we are doing. Sometimes I get the feeling the guards do not want me there, so this speech by the warden was reassuring.

I also met and had a lengthy conversation with a man named Chuck McLaurin. He has written a book called *Spiritual Truths* and he gave me a copy.

On December 3, 1982, he was involved in an automobile accident that caused him to have an encounter with God that forever changed his life. As he lay dying in Memorial Herman Hospital in Houston, according to him, his spirit left his body and he found himself in the presence of God. At this point, he realized that during his life he had produced very little fruit for the Kingdom of God and he asked the Lord for another chance. God granted him that second chance and Chuck returned to his body on Earth. Since then he has written his book and dedicated his life to ministering the Gospel of Jesus Christ.

Oddly enough, his daughter was also in a severe automobile accident some months back and he had spent almost every waking minute helping her recover. I am not sure why he singled me out to share all of this information but I thank God I had the opportunity to meet him. I am sure our paths will cross again as he ministers on death row as well.

BACK TO MICHAEL HALL

His execution date was a little over two weeks away. As I approached his cell, he was sleeping but when he heard me, he got up so we could talk. He told me that he had been filling out the required paperwork for his execution. When they asked him if he had anybody he wanted to put on his execution list, he named Pastor Wayne from Louisiana.

This is not the first time I have heard about this pastor. Evidently, he makes the trip once a month from Louisiana to Texas to minister to death-row inmates. I hope to meet this pastor someday because most of the inmates seem to like him.

Michael went on to tell me that he was waiting on the results of a mental retardation appeal. I have noticed in our past visits, and this one as well, that he does seem to have problems expressing himself. He has moments when he seems to lose his train of thought and he freezes momentarily. I have no idea if he has mental retardation problems or not.

My primary objective is to ensure that he is a born-again Christian and just for my own curiosity, maybe get some sort of glimpse as to why he committed his crime. I told him I would visit him again next week and asked if I could pray with him. He immediately agreed and after a beautiful prayer for God's mercy and strength, I said my good-byes and moved on.

FEBRUARY 8, 2011

Michael was scheduled to be executed next week on Tuesday, February 15, 2011. As you can imagine, he was a little distant and the mood was a little solemn from when I saw him the week before. He did not have much to say but he did say that his lawyer did not offer him much hope of getting a stay of execution. It finally dawned on me at that moment that I was looking into the eyes of a man who was scheduled to die next week! Somehow, the reality of that was beginning to sink in. I cannot imagine what must be going through his mind. However, things are different now that I know this man. He is humanized in my eyes. After all, regardless of what the world thinks, this is one of God's beloved creatures.

I asked him if I could pray with him one last time and he agreed. I prayed that if he should be executed next week, that it would be a smooth transition. I do not like the word "death." Transition sounds much better and is a precisely accurate term for Christians. I told Michael good-bye, possibly for the last time, and as I was walking away, for some reason, I turned around and said, "I love you, brother."

I was not sure how he was going to take that but he meekly said, "I love you too, BroJack." I had to turn away as a heavy sadness came over me while I moved to the next inmate.

FEBRUARY 15, 2011

Today the chaplains were locked out of death row because Michael was set to be executed sometime after 6:00 p.m. There will be no more conversations with Michael on this earth.

*UPDATE: Michael Wayne Hall — 2/15/2011

Michael Wayne Hall, 31, received lethal injection less than an hour after the U.S. Supreme Court refused to stop his punishment for the abduction and murder of Amy Robinson. Hall was pronounced dead at 6:23 p.m. at the Huntsville Unit of the Texas Department of Criminal Justice.

HIS OFFICIAL LAST STATEMENT:

First of all I would like to give my sincere apology to Amy's family. We caused a lot of heartache, grief, pain and suffering, and I am sorry. I know it won't bring her back. I would like to sing, I would like to sing for that person's dead. The old is gone. I am not the same person that I used to be; that person is dead. It's up to you if you would find it in your heart to forgive. As for my family, I am sorry I let you down. I caused a lot of heartache, and I ask for your forgiveness. I am not crying for myself; I am crying for the lost and those that are dying for their sins, those that are committing suicide, those that don't know God and have never been set free. I've been locked up thirteen years. I am not locked up inside; all of these years I have been free. Christ has changed me. Even though I have to die for my mistake, He paid for mine by wages I could never pay. Here I am a big strong youngster, crying like a baby. I am man enough to show my emotions and I am sorry. I am sorry for everything. I wish I could take it back, but I can't.

BROJACK'S FINAL COMMENTS:

Exactly thirteen years to the day that Michael committed his crime, he was executed. This was my first execution experience and I had a hard time processing it. I liked Michael and I will miss my visits with him.

However, I believe justice was served today, but I am just not sure whose justice it was. I spent the last few months talking and praying with a man who is now gone from this Earth forever. The reality of that has shocked my system. Also let's not forget that there is a victim's family out there that will never get to see their loved one again as well. I feel that, in this situation, there are no winners, only tragedy. My prayers are with Michael's family as well as the victim's.

Why did Michael commit this horrible crime? I would have to say it was out of *ignorance*. He did not have a relationship with God when he committed his crime. Without the Holy Spirit of God dwelling in the hearts of His believers, I believe we are capable of pretty much anything. I also believe Michael knew what he was doing but probably did not understand how cruel and wrong it really was at the time because he had no relationship with God. It is so sad but it took him coming to death row to find God and to realize just what he had done.

Did Michael die as a new creature in Christ? Had he truly given his life to Jesus Christ and become a new person on the inside? Only God Almighty and Michael know that for sure. However, based on his actions, his comments, and his professed faith in Jesus, the Bible says he is now with God in heaven. *For God so loved the world that He gave His only Son, that whoever believes in Him shall not perish but have everlasting life (John 3:16).* Amen.

Chapter 6

Christianity and Murder?

Train up a child in the ways he should go,
and when he is old he will not turn from it.
~ Proverbs 22:6 ~

Timothy Adams, Inmate # 999448

This chapter's Bible verse from Proverbs says when a parent teaches a child to make the right decisions, the child will choose the right way. This is somewhat puzzling to me because of stories like that of Timothy Adams. He murdered his own nineteen- month-old son and yet according to him, he was raised a born again Christian. How can you have the Holy Spirit of God inside your heart and commit such a horrible act as murdering your own son? Maybe our interaction with Timothy can help us understand.

CRIME CONVICTION: On February 20, 2002, in Houston, Texas, Timothy Adams shot his nineteen-month-old black male child twice in the chest, resulting in his death. His attorneys maintained the shooting occurred during an emotional crisis brought on by news that his wife intended to leave him. He has an execution date of February 22, 2011.

DECEMBER 14, 2010

Today I spoke with Timothy Adams for the first time. I was concerned about talking to this inmate considering the nature of his crime. I was not sure if my feelings about what he had done to his defenseless son were going to shine through in my speech or body language. Nevertheless, as I approached his cell I felt like God reminded me of why I was there in the first place and that it is not for me to judge.

For your information, I try to research each inmate's crime before I meet them, so I don't say something stupid. For example, if I asked Timothy if he had any children, trying to break the ice to start a conversation, due to the nature of his crime that could have quickly ended any chance of me presenting the Gospel to him.

I had been walking by Timothy's cell and speaking to him with no results until today. For some reason today was the day he decided to speak to Brojack! I never want to push myself on anyone so I always let the inmate decide if they want to talk to me.

Timothy was a large black man and he had a toothpick in one corner of his mouth and a smirk on his face as I approached him. He had on his prison whites and his cell appeared very organized.

He seemed reluctant at first, but as the conversation went on, he began to loosen up. I saw a Bible on Timothy's shelf so I asked him how often he read it. It was at this point I found out that he was raised in church and has believed in God since he was eight years old. He talked about a scripture in the book of Daniel that explains how God judges the insides of a man, not the outward appearance. I then told him how Romans 10:9 goes along with the verse he referenced. This was a good sign in that we were already talking about God's Word!

I enjoyed our visit but at this point, I am not sure about his sincerity. He constantly had this smirk on his face, which made it hard to tell if he was being serious or trying to play mind games. I will go back to visit him next week with a different approach that I will rely on God to give me. I thanked him for his time, which seemed to take him by surprise. I do not think he is used to someone showing him respect.

DECEMBER 28, 2010

Today I was blessed to have a chaplain escort me over to death row and on the way there he asked me if I have been successful talking with Timothy Adams. He had heard through the prison grapevine that I was talking to him last week. He said in the past they could not get him to talk. I told him that I briefly talked to him for the first time last week and that he was apprehensive at first, but opened up after we started talking about the Bible and different scriptures. The chaplain seemed shocked and asked me to keep him updated on my interactions with Timothy. I said sure, but did not understand why until I later found out that I was the only Chaplain he ever talked to on death row.

After getting my escort and arriving on the deathwatch section of death row, to my joy, Timothy was smiling when I approached his cell. We had not been talking very long when he got his Bible out and started talking about different scriptures again. After we had a brief Bible study, I decided to change the subject in hopes of getting to know him better.

I asked him if he had many visits from family members since he has been on the row. He said his family has been very supportive throughout this whole ordeal, especially his dad. He told me his father was a Pentecostal preacher in Houston and comes to see him every week. Timothy had told me on my first visit that he was raised in the church but

I did not realize his father was a preacher. I was thinking to myself that he must be a good Christian and a good father because even though his son was responsible for the death of a nineteen-month-old child (his grandson, by the way), he did not condemn him or forsake him. That is what Jesus would do, forgive him. Still, I know his dad's heart had to be broken. I think at this point I can rule out a troubled childhood as being the motive behind Timothy's crime.

I asked Timothy if I could pray with him and to my excitement, he agreed. After we prayed, I thanked him for talking to me. Most inmates are shocked when I thank them. However, as I said before, it is all about respect in prison. Even on the row.

FEBRUARY 1, 2011

Today Timothy was not in his regular cell so I turned to the guard and asked what happened to him. He said he was moved upstairs on the second tier but that he does not talk to anyone. He proceeded to tell me that for the first couple of years, Timothy did not even come out of his cell and he spoke to no one. I told the guard that I have already talked to him twice. The guard was insistent that Timothy talks to no one. I asked him to take me to his cell to make sure we were talking about the same inmate.

As I approached Timothy's cell, he was sleeping on the floor with his head leaning against his cell door. I thought this was odd but quickly remembered nothing is surprising on the row. When Timothy heard my voice, he got up. I asked him if he felt like talking today and he said yes.

I then asked him what we talked about the last time I saw him and he smiled that sheepish grin he had and then said he remembered he was educating me on some scripture in the book of Daniel. I briefly looked around to the guard and *his jaw was hanging open!* I guess he was surprised. So much for Timothy not talking to anyone. Apparently, the guard did not know that with man things are impossible but with God all things are possible (Matthew 19:26). Amen?

I asked Timothy if his father, who I remembered was a Pentecostal preacher in Houston, had been to visit. He said he comes every week. Then Timothy shared something personal. He said he had not shared this with anyone before. I was very excited because maybe this would give me some insight as to why he committed his horrible crime, which would in turn help me understand this horrible sin called murder.

Timothy proceeded to tell me that throughout this whole ordeal, as he put it, there had been one person who has stuck by him the entire time. Not condoning his crime but supporting him spiritually. It was his old boss.

When he committed the crime that landed him here on the row, he was a security guard and his boss was a woman who had always treated him right. Through these last seven years that he had been on the row, she remained in contact and tried to encourage and comfort him as much as possible. He was very appreciative of that. I told him that she must be a special person and he was blessed to have her in his life.

As our visit ended, I told him I would be back and thanked him for talking to me. He smiled and said, "I'll be here BroJack, but not for long." I knew what he meant.

FEBRUARY 8, 2011

Today again, to the surprise of the guards, Timothy was more than willing to talk to me. I asked if his father had been to see him and he said the bad weather in Houston kept him away last week. He talked about the paperwork he has been filling out concerning his execution. I remembered Michael Hall talking about the same paperwork.

There is one question I desperately wanted to ask Timothy but I could not bring myself to do it. I wanted to know why he shot his nineteen-month-old son twice in the chest. The court documents said he did it to punish his wife who threatened to leave him. I wanted to ask him why he shot his son instead of shooting her, but I have to remember that God has not sent me there for that purpose. I am there for one primary reason and that is to tell Timothy about the loving grace of Jesus Christ and how he can accept that grace and be saved if he has not already.

Timothy and I talked a little longer than usual and then I asked if he would allow me to pray for him and he agreed again. I do not know why but I am always surprised when an inmate agrees to prayer. I guess in my judgmental mind I see them as cold-hearted people who want nothing to do with God. However, I am quickly finding out that is generally not the case. After our prayer as I was turning to walk away, for some reason I could not stop myself from saying to him, "I love you brother."

He gave me his sheepish grin and said, "I love you too, BroJack." He held up two fingers and said, "Two weeks, brother." I just smiled in acknowledgment and moved to the next inmate. I am not sure why I have started telling certain inmates that I love them as a brother in Christ, but I am sure that is what Jesus would have done and as His representative in there, I need to do the same thing. I had a bad feeling that I have talked to Timothy for the last time. It is becoming harder and harder to tell these inmates good-bye.

FEBRUARY 22, 2011

Today the warden decided to lock down death row because Timothy Adams was set to be executed sometime after 6:00 p.m. Sometimes he does that to reduce the possibility of someone getting hurt because he knows this is a bad time on the row. All inmates know when someone goes out to be executed. The prison grapevine is swift.

*UPDATE: TIMOTHY WAYNE ADAMS

Timothy Wayne Adams, convicted of killing his nineteen-month-old son, was executed at the Texas State Penitentiary in Huntsville. Adams, who never denied killing his son in February, 2002, offered no final statement before his death by lethal injection Tuesday, February 22, 2011, *The Houston Chronicle* reported. Adams, 42, shot his son, Timothy Adams Jr., during a 2 1/2-hour standoff with police at his home. His attorneys maintained the shooting occurred during an emotional crisis brought on by news that his wife intended to leave him. His attorneys said their client had no prior criminal record and was an exemplary prisoner during his seven years on death row. In the witness room, Adams's mother, Wilma Adams, repeated, "He's going to sleep. He's going to sleep. He's going to a better place. He's going to get to see Jesus," the *Chronicle* said. As Adams's execution date neared, members of his family and church appealed to the Texas Board of Pardons and Paroles, the newspaper said. The board rejected the inmate's appeal Friday. Adams' appeal to the U.S. Supreme Court mirrored a failed appeal to the Texas Court of Criminal Appeals. The federal high court rejected his appeal several hours after it received it Tuesday.

HIS OFFICIAL LAST STATEMENT: No final statement offered.

BROJACK'S FINAL COMMENTS:

I do not care what anybody says; you cannot share the Gospel of Jesus Christ with a man and not get to know him a little. I felt as though I knew Timothy as well as anyone because we shared the same God and we both understood the importance of knowing and accepting Jesus Christ as our Lord and Savior.

I will never forget my last encounter with Timothy. I will never forget the smile on his face as he said good-bye while holding up two fingers, indicating that in two weeks he would be with God. I cannot begin to know what was truly in his mind and heart, but his outward appearance almost seemed relieved that his time on this Earth was about to end.

I was not surprised to hear that Timothy did not make a final statement. Everyone on the row told me that he rarely spoke to anyone. I do not know why he chose me to finally open up to, but I hope that God, working through me, gave him some sort of comfort.

After spending a few months with Timothy, I am still no closer to understanding why a professed Christian committed the murder of his own son. If I have to label it by the world's standards, I would call this a *crime of passion*. He was so upset at the prospect of losing his son through divorce, that he was willing to sacrifice him as well as himself.

There is one thing that does stand out in this scenario. Before Timothy created his crime of murder, he had gotten away from the church and his relationship with God had almost disappeared. I think remaining surrounded by Godly things in a lost world will definitely help a person make right decisions. Remaining righteous (or in right standing) with God is the key. If you fill your heart with the things of this world, it will not be long before the things of this world will allow you to murder your own son! Such was the case of Timothy Adams.

It is still so hard to understand Timothy's terrible act, just as it is still hard to understand why that man killed my mother. The Bible says in Deuteronomy 29:29, *The secret things belong to God but the things revealed belong to us and our children.*" We need to be careful about trying to understand everything about God and to concentrate on the things God has chosen to reveal to us. I will see Timothy again, at the throne of God someday and I believe we will not remember how we knew each other, only that we did. Amen!

Chapter 7

Sexual Crime

But if out in the country a man happens to meet a girl pledged to be married and rapes her, only the man who has done this shall die.
~ Deuteronomy 22:25~

Humberto Leal, Inmate #999162

This chapter's Bible verse deals with rape, and this sin goes on throughout the world and touches almost every community. In Texas, the penalty for rape that results in murder is death. Praise God, if you are saved and no matter what you have done, God will accept you into His Kingdom. However, you will still more than likely suffer the consequences of your sins while you are still on Earth, Christian or not. Sometimes people think that when they find salvation they will then be free from man's punishment. In most cases, you will still be held accountable, as was the case of Humberto Leal.

I am convinced almost all crimes or sins have some underlying connection to sex. It is the most powerful weapon satan has in his arsenal. I think we forget sometimes that it was God who created sex. It was meant to be a wonderful experience between a man and a woman. However, man and satan have turned it into something evil and dirty. Everyone is affected by it eventually, in one form or another. What makes a person like Humberto Leal take their sexual desires to the point of murder? Maybe Humberto can give us a clue.

CRIME CONVICTION: Humberto Leal was convicted of the abduction, rape, and bludgeoning death of sixteen-year-old Adria Saveda of San Antonio, Texas. Saveda was raped with a piece of lumber and her head crushed by a thirty-five pound piece of asphalt after being abducted from a party by Leal. Her nude body was found near a creek with a piece of lumber still protruding from her vagina. When arrested, police found cuts and scratches on Leal's face and body.

DECEMBER 21, 2010

Today I met Humberto Leal for the first time. As I was talking to another inmate, a guard came to me and told me that the inmate at the end of the row wanted to meet me. That can be a good thing or a bad thing, depending on their motive. However, that's why I am here, so I made him my next stop. It does feels kind of good when an inmate asks to see you.

I recognized Humberto's name from the prison website, as an inmate on the row who had an execution date. As I mentioned earlier, every week before I go to death row I check the Texas Department of Criminal Justice website to see who is on death watch. Death watch is a special section of death row where inmates with execution dates are housed. These cells have two cameras that monitor the inmates twenty-four hours a day, seven days a week, until they are taken to Huntsville for their execution.

In addition to learning about their crimes, I do this website check so I can plan to visit those inmates who have an execution coming soon. I had plans to visit Humberto later because his date was not until July 7, 2011, and I was concentrating on spending more time with inmates who had sooner dates. However, I will not turn down anyone who wants to talk to me.

At first glance, Humberto did not appear friendly. I immediately started to question why he wanted to talk to me. By the look in his eyes, I think he was sizing me up. I introduced myself as a volunteer chaplain and asked how he was doing.

After talking to him briefly, I found a way to bring Jesus into the conversation. I looked around his cell for some sign that he might be a Christian or at the least might know about God. I saw a Bible on his shelf, so I used that to break into a conversation about Jesus. When I asked what kind of Bible he had, he instantly proclaimed that he was saved and knew exactly where he was going when he died. Wow! I was not expecting that but I'll take it! He went on to tell me that when he was given his execution date last month by the judge, he experienced nothing but peace. He explained that peace could only come from God.

I felt as though he was finished sizing me up and was getting tired of our conversation so I asked if he would like for me to come back next week and he said he would like that a lot. I thanked him for taking time to talk with me and he said it was his pleasure.

At this point, I am not sure if Humberto is saved or if he is just telling me what he thinks a preacher would want to hear. I believe the Holy Spirit will show me where his heart is sooner or later and maybe give me some insight as to why he would do such a horrible thing to a young girl.

As I was walking down the stairs to the lower tier he shouted, "Thank you, BroJack." That is short for Brother Jack and, in case you were wondering, that is what the inmates were starting to call me throughout death row. I have found out it does not take long for word to spread on the row. I turned and said, "No Thank you!"

DECEMBER 28, 2010

Today was very busy on the row and I was running out of time because of other visits, as I came to Humberto's cell. I visited with him for the first time last week and he told me he was saved, so this time I wanted to dig deeper and make sure he knew what that meant.

After a few pleasantries, I dived right in with, "How is your walk with Jesus today?"

He said the same as it was yesterday and the same way it will be tomorrow. Good! I gave him Romans 10:9 to study this week and told him we would talk about it during our next visit. I have learned that those inmates who profess to know Jesus get excited when they are asked to discuss the Bible, especially with a preacher. It gives them a sense of purpose.

I asked if I could pray with him and he agreed. So far, everyone who I have asked has been very willing to pray with me. I thanked him and told him I would see him next week. I explained to him that because others have sooner execution dates I needed to spend more time with them. He said he fully understood.

However, just as I ended my prayer, I lost my escort so I was taken out of death row and through general population (G-pop) on my way to freedom. Praise God, I can walk out of there, but more importantly, praise God for the opportunity to minister to those inmates. Amen!

FEBRUARY 1, 2011

It has been awhile since I have spoken to Humberto because he has either been gone from his cell for whatever reason or been asleep when I came by. When I finally got to his cell today he was cooking something and was just about to sit down and eat, so I cut my visit short. Mealtime is a very important time to the inmates so I try not to interrupt during this time. You are probably wondering how a death row inmate could be cooking in his cell. I'll just say this, when a man is locked in a cell 24 hours a day he can come up with some very ingenious ways to get things done. It is not my place to give away trade secrets. That is not my purpose on the row. I told him I would be back soon and he seemed fine with that. His execution date is July 7, 2011, so I have time to visit with him more in the future.

FEBRUARY 8, 2011

You have to catch Humberto at just the right time in order to get him to talk. Today he seemed to be in a good mood. I asked how he was doing and he just smiled and said, "All right, I guess."

As you can guess by his name, he is from Mexico. I do not know how, but our conversation switched to hot sauce and jalapenos. He had bottles of hot sauce lined up in his cell. I asked him how his stomach could take such a harsh mixture of hot sauce and jalapenos and he replied, "I have been eating them since a child and they do not bother me." I felt like this was my opportunity to dig into his childhood without seeming to pry. However, when I asked about his childhood, his demeanor suddenly changed. He seemed agitated so I thought it better to change the subject. I did learn from his reaction that there must be some bad memories for him in his past. Perhaps in one of our later visits he will decide to share some of them. Maybe I would get a clue as to why he viciously murdered an innocent young girl.

I changed the subject back to jalapenos and I told him they did not sit well with me and that I have never eaten a whole one. He showed me several empty bags of jalapenos he had eaten that day alone. He confessed however that sometimes he has a little trouble in that they burn both cheeks (he meant, mouth cheeks or butt cheeks? All right, forget it!). I thought that was funny so we laughed awhile. It always makes my heart sing when I am able to laugh with these condemned men.

I thanked him for talking to me and I moved on. I feel like Humberto is starting to feel more comfortable with me, so next time I plan to talk more about Jesus. Gaining an inmate's confidence can be a slow process sometimes but it is essential to take your time because it does not take much to alienate them. One wrong word and it is over.

MARCH 15, 2011

Today Humberto was gone from his cell so I did not see him but on a side note, there were many other things happening on the row today. There was an unusual amount of tension. One of the guards told me there had already been eight mace incidents that afternoon alone and they were getting ready for their special team to do an extraction. Evidently, an inmate refused to leave his cell. It did not take me long to find out the problem.

There had been a change in the shower policy that had many of the inmates very upset. Only one inmate is allowed in the shower cell at a time on death row. There is a metal door just like the ones on their cells that has a trap door in the middle of it. The trap door (or bean trap as it is called) on the cell door is used to give the inmates food but on the shower door it is opened to allow steam to escape. This allows the inmate to take a longer shower. For whatever reason, it was decided that the trap door was now to be closed, not allowing steam to escape thus shortening the inmate's showers. It may not seem like a big deal to us but to them it was monumental and the inmates were mad! I decided to be extra careful during my visits today!

APRIL 19, 2011

Today before I went to the row, I found out that the person who got me started visiting death row got hurt on his job. He is in the construction business and apparently fell off a roof during a job. He called me Sunday night from the hospital and told about his injury. I feel so bad for him. He broke most of the ribs on his right side and part of his pelvis. I went to the hospital Monday and he was in very bad shape. He showed me a bruise that ran from under his arm all the way down to his knee. I have never seen such a deep, dark bruise. He had a tube stuck in his nose that ran into his stomach to helped drain excess fluids. I felt so sorry for my friend. He will take a long time to heal and then there will be extensive rehabilitation. He said he is supposed to walk on a walker in the beginning. My prayers are with him and his wife.

Today as I headed to A pod (death watch) the guard said something to me that touched my heart. He said, "I know you need to get to A pod but there are a lot of inmates on the other pods who are asking to talk with you. What should I tell them?"

I said, "Just tell them I need to spend a majority of my time with inmates on death watch and I think most of them will understand."

He said, "Okay, I'll tell them."

This made me feel good because all of those inmates know why I am there. They know I am going to bring up the name of Jesus sooner or later and they know I can't give them anything or take anything from them. As a volunteer chaplain, I cannot even associate with any of their family members. So for them to willingly want to talk to me, knowing those circumstances and restrictions, touches my heart.

It has been a long time since I have been able to spend any quality time with Humberto but today was different. Usually Humberto is asleep when I come by but this time he was waiting on me. He said he had gotten in a little trouble and they took his prize possession away, his radio. I could tell he was lost without it. This was probably a good thing because he had his Bible in his hand and he wanted to talk to me. All right! This is what I like to see!

He was reading Revelation chapter 6:1–2. He was trying to figure out who the horsemen were that God was talking about in these verses. We went back and forth on the interpretation but it was good healthy discussions and he was having fun. I wanted to spend more time with him but my time was running out. I had already been on the row two and a half hours talking to other inmates.

As I was leaving, Humberto issued me a challenge. He wanted me to find out a more common word for "avocado." I told him I will have his answer next week. I prayed with Humberto and felt like we had a great visit. I feel we are as close as we are going to get, so I am happy. Maybe in my future visits I can find out why he committed his crime.

APRIL 17, 2011

Today, when I got to Humberto's cell I could see he was asleep so I thought maybe I should not disturb him. As I turned to leave, he jumped out of his rack and started immediately talking to me. It used to be when I first came on the row that if an inmate was in his rack he would not talk to me but now I notice if they see me they will get up.

Humberto was such a case. I started with the usual pleasantries and then I reminded him of the questions he had for me the last time I saw him. He seemed surprised that I remembered. The first one was, "What's another name for avocado?" I had to look it up on the internet but I had the answer.

I said, "The answer is alligator pear." He seemed happy that I took his questions seriously.

Then he said, "What about Revelation 6:1? Who was riding those horses?"

I had done my research and explained to him about how each of the four horsemen represented a punishment that God put upon the Earth during the Tribulation period.

He seemed really excited with that answer and I felt we were going to get into a good theological discussion but just then I heard the guards running out of A pod and I knew I was about to lose my escort. When that happens, it means one or more of the inmates are causing trouble on the row and most of the guards head for the disturbance.

I said a quick good-bye to Humberto and just like that my time on the row was finished for the day. This is why every moment with an inmate is so precious. Your time with them can end at any moment. I made my way to the main gate and I was a free man again! Praise God Almighty for my freedom!

JUNE 6, 2011

Today I am trying a different day. Recently I had a meeting with the warden, and he suggested I change my visitation day from Tuesday to Wednesday. He said that I would have a better chance of getting an escort on Wednesdays because all visitations are stopped at noon. It is Media Visitation day and many guards are freed up. And, sure enough, I had no problem getting a ride to the row today or getting an escort to the pods.

Things seemed calm on the row but I think it was because it was an execution day. John Balentine was scheduled to be executed at 6:00 p.m. Lee Taylor was supposed to be executed tomorrow. It used to be they would lockdown the prison on executions days but lately they have not been doing that. You can sense the change in the atmosphere when a fellow inmate has gone to the death chamber in Huntsville. Everyone on death row knows all about it. Back-to-back executions create an especially tense and dangerous atmosphere on the row.

I have not seen Humberto in a while but I could tell my visit with him was going to be good today because before I could get to his cell he was calling for me from his door. When I got to his cell, he started out by getting on to me because I had not been by to see him in a few weeks. He said he heard me on the pod but I did not come to see him. I told him that I came by once and he was asleep and another time I lost my escort before I could get to him. This was good news because it meant that he had missed our visits. He seemed satisfied with my answers and asked how I had been. I told him I survived one day at a time and he said, "I know what you mean."

I asked him how he was doing and he said, "I am ready to go. I have made my peace with God and have asked everyone to forgive me. That is all I can do. I am ready to suffer the consequences for what I did." I asked him to get his Bible and read Romans 8:18 to me. He read, *I consider that our present sufferings are not worth comparing with the glory that will be revealed in us.*

When he finished I explained that this verse meant that no matter what we are going through on this Earth it cannot be compared to what God has waiting for us in heaven. Humberto smiled and said, "That's good, man."

Then he got a serious look on his face and said, "Tell me which one of God's creatures was not allowed on the Ark?"

I said I had no idea. He replied, "Termites" and began laughing. Here is a man who has a few weeks to live and he is telling jokes! That tells me his faith in God is where it needs to be. He asked me to repeat the verse I quoted to him last time we talked and I really had to reach but I remembered: Revelation 12:11, *They overcame him by the blood of the lamb and by the word of their testimony; and they did not love their lives until the death.*

He just smiled after I quoted it and said, "I hear ya, BroJack."

Just then, I remembered that God had given me eight verses to give to Humberto and this was my chance. I gave him Revelation 2:7, 2:11, 2:17, 2:26, 3:5, 3:12, 3:21, and 21:7. In these verses, God lists some wonderful things that He has waiting for us when we get to heaven. I was hoping that this information from God would comfort him in some way.

My time was running short so I prayed with Humberto and moved on to see if I could talk to Milton Mathis, possibly for the last time. Milton was another inmate who was scheduled to be executed next week.

I had done some research on Humberto and supposedly he was abused as a child and sexually abused by a priest. It had also been reported that he suffered permanent brain damage in his frontal lobe. I do not know about the sexual abuse but he appears to be somewhat intelligent based on our conversations. He has no problem that I can see, understanding the Word of God. However, it is not uncommon for people who have been sexually abused to commit sexual crimes. I do not know for sure but maybe that is where Humberto got the urge to rape and kill.

JUNE 29, 2011

Today I have a sense of urgency to visit with Humberto because he is scheduled to be executed next week.

I immediately asked him if he had a chance to read those verses I had given him the last time we spoke. He said he had been reading them constantly all week. He was very thankful that I had given them to him. I asked if he had heard anything about his case and he said no.

He looked me straight in the eyes and said, "I am ready to go, BroJack. I don't want a stay of execution. I have been in this steel box living like an animal for sixteen years. I don't want to live like this anymore. I know I am going to be with God in heaven so I say let's get this show on the road."

I smiled and said, "God bless you, brother. I pray for God's grace and mercy upon you."

I don't know what will happen to Humberto next week but I strongly feel that if the State of Texas executes him he will be in the presence of the Lord.

He looked at me and said, "Remember, if God ever calls you to build an Ark, leave the termites out!" I laughed out loud so I would not cry.

I prayed with Humberto, possibly for the last time on this Earth. How do you say good-bye to a man who is scheduled to be executed next week?

JULY 5, 2011

Today is Monday, July 5th, and I received a phone call from the prison telling me that the prison is on lockdown and may be that way for several weeks. That means I will not see Humberto Leal on this Earth again if he is executed this Wednesday, July 7th. I am very thankful that I have been giving him scriptures over the last few weeks to provide him comfort in this stressful time of his life.

*UPDATE: HUMBERTO LEAL, JULY 07, 2011

MEXICAN NATIONAL SHOUTS 'VIVA MEXICO!' AS HE'S EXECUTED IN TEXAS

As the lethal injection began taking effect, the Mexican National convicted of the brutal rape and killing of a teenage girl in 1995 shouted, "Viva Mexico!" just before he died at a Texas prison.

Efforts by Humberto Leal's attorneys to halt the execution fell short, with the US Supreme Court turning back a stay request and Texas Governor Rick Perry refusing to grant a pardon. He was pronounced dead at 6:21 p.m. local time.

http://en.wikipedia.org/wiki/Humberto_Leal_Garcia

HIS OFFICIAL LAST STATEMENT:

I am sorry for everything that I have done. I have hurt many people. For years, I have never thought that I deserved any type of forgiveness. Lord Jesus Christ in my life, I know He has forgiven me, I have accepted His forgiveness. I have accepted everything. Let this be final and be done. I take the full blame for this. I am sorry and forgive me. I am truly sorry. I ask for forgiveness. Life goes on and it surely does.

I am sorry for the victim's family for what I had did. May they forgive me. I do not know if you believe me, life goes on. I am sure it does. To the man to the right of me, I ask for forgiveness for you. Life goes on, it surely does. I ask for forgiveness. I am truly sorry. That is all. Let's get this show on the road. One more thing, Viva Mexico, Viva Mexico.

BROJACK'S FINAL COMMENTS:

There was a lot of controversy around Humberto's execution. According to a national treaty between Mexico and the United States, as a Mexican national, he was entitled to assistance from the Mexican consul. However, at the time of his arrest, he did not reveal his Mexican citizenship, and the issue of consular access was not raised during the trial. A 2004 ruling by the International Court of Justice [in *Avena and Other Mexican Nationals (Mexico v. United States of America)*] found that he and about fifty other Mexican nationals condemned to execution in the United States had been denied their right under the Vienna Convention to be told that they may contact their consular officials. A 2008 Supreme Court decision declared the international court's decision binding, but said that it was necessary that Congress pass a law obliging states to comply.

As the date scheduled for Leal's execution approached, the Obama administration made a number of comments concerning the execution, saying that it would cause "irreparable harm" to US interests abroad, including the demonstration of "respect for the international rule of law," and would "have serious repercussions for United States foreign relations, law enforcement and other cooperation with Mexico, and the ability of American citizens traveling abroad to have the benefits of consular assistance in the event of detention."

The administration submitted a thirty-page brief to the Supreme Court asking them to stay Leal's execution while Congress considered legislation relating to the right of foreign nationals on death row to contact their consulate for legal aid. On July 7, 2011, the court ruled 5 to 4 that Congress had had adequate time to do so, and wrote in an unsigned majority opinion that it would not "prohibit a state from carrying out a lawful judgment in light of un-enacted legislation." Justice Stephen G. Breyer, in his dissent, which the other three dissenting justices joined, wrote that the execution would damage American foreign policy interests and that the court should defer to the executive branch's traditional prerogative with regard to foreign relations.

Despite calls from US President Barack Obama, the US State Department, and Mexico to the state of Texas for a last-minute reprieve, Leal was executed by lethal injection as scheduled on July 7, 2011.

On July 8, a spokesman for Texas Governor Rick Perry stated, "If you commit the most heinous of crimes in Texas, you can expect to face the ultimate penalty under our laws."

Arturo Sarukhan, Mexico's ambassador to the United States, said that "the government of Mexico has never called into question the heinous nature of the crimes attributed to Mr. Leal and in no way condones violent crime," but condemned the execution; Sarukhan had earlier tried to contact Perry, who would not take his call.

The message: If you are going to kill someone in Texas be prepared to die. It is as simple as that. Also, remember that accepting God's gift of salvation does not exclude you from the secular consequences of your crimes. More than likely, you will pay at the hands of your fellow man. Such was the message of David in the Bible and such is the message of Humberto Leal on death row in Texas.

I will miss Humberto, but I feel I fulfilled my mission, which was to present the Gospel of Jesus Christ to him. What he did with it is between him and God. May God have mercy on him.

Why did he commit the crime that cost him his life and the life of a beautiful, innocent girl? Although we never directly talked about his crime, I believe that a combination of *childhood abuse, alcohol, drugs,* and *lust* brought Humberto to the point where he was capable of committing this terrible crime. I am convinced this deadly combination is responsible for more crimes on this Earth than any other. People will do things while under the influence of drugs and alcohol that they would not dream of doing otherwise. Trust me, I know firsthand!

On a side note, the crazy fact about alcohol and drugs is that we seem to be in a war against drugs but we glorify and encourage alcohol use. All you have to do is watch television for about five minutes to see alcohol consumption advertised as an acceptable form of entertainment. However, we all know that alcohol can be as deadly as other drugs. Where is the logic?

Chapter 8

Justifying Your Sin

There is a way that seems right to man,
but in the end it leads to death.
~ Proverbs 14:12 ~

Mark Stroman, Inmate # 99940

Sometimes when we make decisions, they seem so right at the time. It is partly because so many things bias our rationale. Our environment, and what we learn from others, can be very influential in our decision-making. Such was the case with Mark Stroman.

After spending a lot of time with Mark, I am almost positive that when he committed his crimes, he was sure he was doing the right thing. It was not until he invited Jesus into his life that he was able to see the truth about what he had done. This is a very common theme on death row. After reading about my interactions with Mark, see if you agree.

CRIME CONVICTION: On October 4, 2001, in Mesquite, TX. Stroman murdered a forty-nine-year-old Middle Eastern male convenience store employee during an attempted robbery.

JANUARY 11, 2011

Today I met Mark Stroman for the first time. It was a rough day on death row because Cleve (Sarge) Foster, who we will talk about in the last chapter, was scheduled to be executed today. I had to try to put that out of my mind in order to be an effective witness to the other inmates on the row.

Mark was a very matter-of-fact guy. I did not know it at the time but we were about to become good friends. There were no secrets with him. His cell was different from others I have seen in that he had orange colored light bulbs in his lamps. It gave his cell an eerie orange glow.

I introduced myself and asked if he would like to talk. He said sure and after he commented that he liked my name (BroJack), he immediately started talking about himself.

Almost all of the other inmates I have encountered so far have not mentioned their crime, except for Sarge because he claims he is innocent, but this guy Mark takes full responsibility for his actions and does not deny what he did at all. He seems to have no remorse because he feels his actions were justified. Little did I know my initial snap judgment would be wrong.

When Mark was talking to me that first day, he had such excitement and passion in his facial expressions and voice. You could tell that he believed with all his heart the things he was saying. He seemed very happy for a man who was condemned to die soon.

He started telling me that his sister was in one of the Twin Towers on 9/11 and died because of the attacks on those buildings. According to him, as an act of defending his country, he retaliated by finding the first "towel head" (his words for a person of Middle Eastern descent) he could and killing them. He said he was only defending his constitutional right to defend himself and his country. He was not afraid to die and that in reality he was just waiting his turn. This is one guy I definitely need to revisit to talk about his salvation! He was too pumped up after explaining his story to talk about that on the first visit, but I knew I would be back.

We said our good-byes and I thanked Mark for talking to me. On my way home, I was already beginning to think that Mark's crime was going to be one of *revenge.*

TROUBLE AT THE MAIN GATE
MARCH 15, 2011

As I have mentioned before, when you drive onto the property of the prison, you have to drive down a long driveway that leads to a guard shack. Until today, I would just tell the guard that I was a volunteer chaplain and they would wave me on. Not today! Today I got the full treatment. In my training, before I could qualify to enter the prison, they talked about the search you would experience when you drove onto prison property. I often wondered why no one had ever searched me but today it was my turn in the barrel.

After hearing that I was a chaplain, he said he would have to search my vehicle. He asked me to pop the hood of my car and I realized at this moment that I did not know how. How sad is that! The first thought I had was that this guard was going to think that I was driving a stolen car. After all, who does not know how to open the hood of their car? In my defense, it is a 2010 SUV and I had never had to open the hood. When it is time to change the oil, an indicator on the control panel tells me it's time and I go get an oil change. Gone are the days when you open the hood and check the dipstick to see if your oil level is okay. So there!

Anyway, the guard found the hood release located inside my vehicle and opened the hood. He then proceeded to check the inside of my SUV and as he was looking, he almost jokingly asked if I had any drugs or a gun. I immediately told him that I did have a gun. Just then, it was as if time stood still forever!

He lifted up his head from the back seat and said, "Where is it and do you have a concealed handgun permit."

I thought to myself, *how ironic. I'm going to prison trying to get into prison*! Thank God, I had remembered my training and had locked my gun in the glove compartment before I entered the property. I opened the glove box and showed him the gun. I had one problem though. It is supposed to be unloaded but mine was loaded and ready for action. I started praying, "Please, Lord, don't let him realize that it is loaded."

Just as I finished my prayer, he asked me in passing, "It's not loaded is it?" I remember looking up into the heavens and asking God if He had just heard what I prayed but before I could answer, the guard moved on and did not wait for my answer. I was so relieved because at this point I do not know if I was going to lie to the guard and ask God to forgive me later or just surrender right then and there! After signing his login sheet, the guard told me to be careful and he let me pass. I guarantee you, *next week I will be ready for any inspection!*

BACK TO MY VISIT WITH MARK

Since my last visit with Mark, he had received an execution date of July 20, 2011, a little over four months from now. He did not have an execution date during our first visit so I was anxious to talk to him now that he had his date to see if his attitude about death had changed. The last time I talked to him, he was ready to die and felt no remorse for what he had done.

When he saw me, he said, "What's up, BroJack?"

I said, "Hey, you remembered my name." Then I thought that is a pretty stupid statement considering I might be the only person outside of prison staff that he has talked to in months, maybe years. I made myself a mental note to remember to stop saying that.

Anyway, his attitude was much the same as before. He was upbeat and talked freely about his upcoming execution. He showed no fear and was actually looking forward to his release from this nightmare, as he put it. Mark is the kind of guy you can't help but like, but he also seems like he could be very dangerous given the right circumstances.

I made another mental note to try to see him next week and ask some subtle questions concerning his salvation. He already claims to know Jesus as his Lord and Savior but I am there to try to make sure. He knows me well enough, so soon it will be down to business.

Unfortunately, I cannot spend a lot of time with any one inmate because so many others are starting to ask to talk to me. I told Mark I would see him soon and thanked him for his time.

He replied, "No problem. BroJack. Have a blessed evening."

APRIL 19, 2011

I am starting to get to know Mark about as well as I know Sarge (Cleve) Foster. The one thing I like about Mark is his honesty. He has always been upfront concerning his crime, never denying his actions. I found out earlier that he is convinced he is saved so who am I to dispute him. I still slip a question or two into the conversation every now and then concerning his salvation, just in case.

I told Mark that his friend John King said hello and about how he respected him because of his belief in Jesus. I met John a few weeks ago and he wanted me to relay that message to Mark.

John King, Lawrence Brewer, and Shawn Berry were convicted of dragging James Byrd to death behind their pickup truck in Jasper, Texas. The crime made national news as a hate crime. I told him that John

King said that it is mostly because of him witnessing to him that he is saved today. I could sense the emotions overtaking Mark. Knowing that you helped someone find Jesus is a powerful and emotional feeling.

Then Mark said something that surprised me. He said, "BroJack, my spirituality has prepared me to accept my execution in a few months but my old flesh is starting to get scared." I reminded him of when Jesus was praying in the garden of Gethsemane and His flesh starting getting to Him as well. I told Mark he was in good company. I told him that God would never leave him nor forsake him and that when his time came God would be right there with him. I told him about Sarge's experience, which I will explain completely in the last chapter of this book. Mark smiled and seemed to take comfort in my words.

Then he really surprised me. He asked, "Are you an ordained minister, BroJack?" and I said yes. He said, "I want to know if you would be with me when I am executed?" Just then, a higher sense of reality set in on me. It does not get any more real than this! I wanted to choose my words very carefully here because this condemned man was reaching out to me and I did not want to discourage him.

I said, "Mark, what an honor that you would ask me to be with you and if it is God's will then I will do it. However, I want you to talk to God and make sure it is me that He wants there. And if after praying, God says yes, then I will be there."

Mark said, "You got a deal. We will talk about it more next week." I knew that the warden of Huntsville prison, where the execution chamber is housed, would need time to check out my credentials so we needed to make a final decision next week.

It was time to move on — I could have talked to old Mark the rest of my visit but other guys were shouting out, "BroJack!" So I moved to the next cell.

MAY 3, 2011

Today I headed straight to deathwatch on A pod in hopes that Mark Stroman would be in his cell and, praise God, he was. He had a big smile on his face as he immediately started celebrating the death of Osama Bin Laden. I could see why he was happy because if you remember, according to him, his sister was killed in the 9/11 bombings that were masterminded by Osama Bin Laden. He was killed this week by US forces. That is why Mark started killing what he thought were men of Middle Eastern descent. He killed three and wounded one. Now he faces his own execution July 20th.

No one really wins in this situation. Not only has Mark's family had to deal with the tragic loss of their daughter, now they will have to watch their son be executed by the state of Texas. In addition, there are many family members of Mark's victims suffering as well. Tragic all the way around!

Anyway, we started talking about me being at his execution and I knew it was time for me to give him my answer. So I said, "Mark, if that is what God has put on your heart then I will be there for you if the state will allow me to be your spiritual advisor. But know that I am there to represent Jesus and I hope, through me, He will give you some sort of peace and understanding."

He seemed very pleased and then he said, "BroJack, I want to tell you something. When we see the state chaplains coming, we see an employee of the state, but when we see you coming, we see a man of God." I could not help it. I started to cry and when I looked up tears were welled up in Mark's eyes as well. As our eyes met, we both did the "macho man-up" thing and changed the subject.

I think I said, "What do you think about this weather?"

He said, "It doesn't mean a thing to me!" We both started laughing.

Once again, my time was up on the row and I said my good-byes to Mark. As I was leaving, other inmates were shouting for me but I had to tell them my time was up. I wish I had more time to spend with these guys.

MAY 10, 2011

Last week, Osama Bin Laden was killed. Mark asked me what I thought about him being killed and I told him I had to be honest. When I heard the news of his death, I immediately thought about where he would spend eternity. If he held to his Muslim beliefs to the end then I believe he is currently in a place called Hades destined to be separated from God for eternity. What a horrible thing for anyone to experience.

To my surprise, Mark agreed with me. He said he did not think of that but that he immediately thought about the family he left behind. That was quite a step forward for Mark because, if you remember, it was Osama who masterminded the attack on the World Trade Center towers, the attack that killed Mark's sister. It is also the reason Mark is about to pay the ultimate price, in about two months. I was proud of Mark. I could tell he was actively seeking God.

ROCKIN' THE BOAT

MAY 17, 2011

Before I talk about Mark, I need to tell you about an experience I had last week that I think you will find interesting. Over the course of my life, I have asked myself on several occasions one question: "Why can't I mind my own business and let things run their course without me sticking my big nose in it." Obviously, I haven't gotten an answer because once again I have "agitated the gravel."

It all started last Wednesday when I decided to re-read the training material I received during my certification training to become a volunteer chaplain for the Texas Department of Criminal Justice (TDCJ).

I wanted to make sure I was still compliant and not breaking any prison rules. I do not want to lose my visitation privileges, which can happen very easily. There are many rules that must be followed. While reading the material, I saw a comment that if I had any questions or concerns please contact Volunteer Services, attention Brad Livingston. So in my infinite wisdom I emailed Brad Livingston about the problem with getting escorts on the pods during my visits to death row. Below is my email:

Date: Wed May 11 16:46:54 EDT 2011
From: Jack Williams
To: Brad Livingston
Subject: Polunsky Unit Visitation

Dear Mr. Livingston,

I am a volunteer chaplain and I visit Death Row weekly at the Polunsky Unit in Livingston, Texas. I would like to first say that it has been the most rewarding part of my ministry so far. I was an Associate Pastor for 9 years and now I am starting to evangelize. But visiting the men on Death Row has shown me what ministering is supposed to be like. I firmly believe if Jesus were on Earth today, Death Row would probably be on His schedule. I thank you for allowing me to be a part of this wonderful program. I do have one issue that maybe you can help with. Recently I have been having problems getting an escort on any of the pods. I fully understand that the guards have shower duties to perform and I would not want to get in their way.

I have been thinking of ways to improve the process but have been unsuccessful so far. I go in every Tuesday so maybe I would be more successful on another day. I just feel so bad when I don't get to talk to some of these inmates because they so

desperately need someone to talk to. Any help to resolve this issue
would be greatly appreciated.

God bless
Brother Jack (BroJack)

I sent the email, forgot about it, and went about my business. Yesterday I received a call from the state chaplain at the Polunsky Unit. He wanted to know if I could stop by the warden's office on my way into the prison on Tuesday because the warden had requested to talk with me. I asked what about?

Well, it turns out that Brad Livingston is the Executive Director of the Texas Department of Criminal Justice. Only the Governor of the state of Texas is higher than he is. He had received my email and called the Director of Voluntary Services for the state of Texas who in turn called the warden of the prison. Here we go again! Most people try to stay out of prison and here I am having difficulty trying to stay in. I told the state chaplain I would be happy to talk to the warden. By the way, the chaplain seemed to be very happy that the warden wanted to talk with me because he also has had difficulty getting an escort and he is the state chaplain. He said that maybe some good things would come out of this.

So, after going through the screening process and being signed into the prison, I headed straight for the warden's office. After about five minutes, his secretary came out and apologized because the warden was in a meeting. She said for me to go on to death row and the warden would catch up with me there. So off to the row I go.

The routine lately had been for me to sign in at the main control booth on death row and then proceed by myself to the different pods in hopes of getting an escort on any one of them. Last week, out of three hours I got an escort for fifteen minutes.

However, this time something was different. I asked the guard in the control booth if there were any escorts, fully expecting that she would tell me to try my luck on the pods, but instead she said, "I have an escort for you."

What? I did not say anything but I was very happy. My escort came, asked me where I wanted to go and I immediately said, "A pod, death watch." And just like that I was on death watch. Amen! I have a feeling though that my correspondence with Mr. Livingston had something to do with my ease in getting an escort today!

BACK TO THE ROW

Today Mark was upbeat as usual. If I did not know better I would honestly think he had come to terms with his upcoming execution and not only that he was okay with it, but that he was looking forward to it.

His first comment to me was, "We are still on for July 20th, right?" He was talking about wanting me to be his spiritual advisor during his execution. This is a request that I am not very fond of but I have agreed to it if TDCJ approves. I pray for God's will to be done in this situation. I just smiled and nodded my head yes.

He then asked me if I had a chance to search the website that he had recommended, nomarkministries.org. This website had many end-time prophecies and excerpts from the book of Revelation. I smiled and he immediately knew that I had not.

He said, "Okay, if you do not look at that website before you come back next week, I am going to put a curse on you. Your right testicle will shrink to the size of a BB and your left testicle will swell to the size of a tennis ball."

I shuttered for a moment and then I said, "There is no doubt in my mind that I *will* look at that website as soon as I get home." We both had a good laugh and I indicated that I should step next door to see if an inmate named Gayland Bradford would talk to me. We will meet Gayland in chapter 8.

Mark winked and said, "Go for it, BroJack."

On my way out of the prison, I met the warden and he asked if I had problems getting an escort and I told him no. He smiled at me and said, "Good." That was not much of a meeting but we both knew that in the future the prison staff was going to be more accommodating when it came to providing escorts. I left death row very happy!

MAY 24, 2011

Today, as usual, Mark was waiting on me with that big old grin on his face and we did our usual greeting of bumping fists through the wire-mesh screen in the opening beside his cell door.

I immediately asked if Gayland Bradford was next door and Mark said he was on a two-hour visit. That was good news and bad news. Good in that he was getting a visit but bad for me because he would not be back to his cell until sometime after 5:30 p.m. If I wanted to talk to him I would need to wait, which I fully intended to do because today I was going to try to present the Gospel of Jesus Christ to Gayland.

On the drive up to the prison from Kingwood, I was getting ready. I practiced presenting the Gospel by using the Romans Road (Romans 3:23, 6:23, 5:8, and 10:9). I felt that if I could just present the Gospel to Gayland, then the Holy Spirit would convict and save him. This is my primary objective on death row today. As I said earlier, we will meet Gayland later but I have a sense of urgency because Gayland is a Muslim and he is scheduled to be executed June 1, 2011, just a few weeks from now. I doubt if he will let me present the Gospel because of his religious beliefs, but I was going to try.

I could tell Mark was excited about something so I asked him what was going on. He said, "You are not going to believe this!" — the man who had survived Mark's shooting spree had forgiven him and was now trying to get Mark's death sentence commuted to life.

He went on to describe in detail how the man had survived. He said it was only by mistake that Mark had not killed him. The gun he was using was double-barreled. In one barrel was a 9 mm bullet and in the other barrel was buckshot. A lever on top of the barrels determined which barrel he was going to use. He had it set for the 9 mm bullet but in his excitement he accidentally hit the lever and switched it to buckshot. He said he aimed at the man's head and shot him in the face with the buckshot. The man survived but lost his left eye.

And now the very same man (who is a devout Muslim by the way), was trying to get Mark a lighter sentence of life in prison. Two things amazed me. First, how candidly Mark described shooting this man in the face, after he had already murdered three other men. Secondly, how much forgiveness and mercy this victim had in his heart.

I could not help but wonder if I would have that same forgiveness and mercy if someone shot me in the face, causing permanent damage. As a Christian and a preacher, I would hope so, but no one knows for sure until faced with that challenge.

Mark is definitely something else and I cannot help but like the guy. However, I hope he changes his mind about wanting me as his spiritual advisor during his execution on July 20, 2011. I prayed with him and moved to the next cell to talk with another inmate.

MAY 30, 2011

Today as I walked from the main control station, across the yard into One Building, I saw the Warden sitting on a bench just outside the door. This was the same warden who I thought was not very happy with me because he thought I ran crying to Brad Livingston (Director of Texas prisons) about the difficulty in getting escorts. To my surprise, though, he said, "Hello, preacher" and then told me that death row was on lockdown and would be that way for a week. No one was allowed out of their cells during lockdown except those inmates who are having their cells searched. I asked him if I could still get in and he said yes but that I might have trouble getting an escort because of the lockdown. I said thanks and decided to go to the row anyway.

As soon as I checked in at the death row control booth, I was immediately given an escort. Things were definitely better since my meeting with the warden. The escort asked where I wanted to go and I replied, "A pod, death watch." I headed straight for Mark Stroman's cell.

By now, Mark Stroman had become my first stop. I loved going through the metal door that leads into that section on A pod and seeing him smiling from his cell door. He immediately said that Gayland Bradford was on an all-day visit because of his scheduled execution tomorrow. I told him I would wait around in hopes that I would get to see him one more time.

I asked how Mark was doing and he said, "I have to confess something. I lost the piece of paper that I wrote your full name on." I don't give out my full name to just everyone on the row because even though these inmates are basically in solitary confinement, they can still make something happen to you if they wanted. They can reach outside the walls of the prison or into the general population to put a hit on you and, if they do, it will happen. Most inmates know me only by Brother Jack, or BroJack for short. Mark needed my full name to submit as his spiritual advisor for his execution on July 20, 2011. I am hoping the warden at Huntsville will turn me down for some reason but I do not want Mark to know that. I am not interested in watching him die. As a man of God, I will be there if my presence offers him comfort in his final moments. I whispered my full name and he wrote it down again.

He then started telling me again about the man that he shot in the head, who had survived and is now trying to get Mark's sentence commuted to life. Mark said he forgot to tell me something last week even more bizarre about this situation. He said that after he killed three men and wounded one more, his plan was to head to this Muslim mosque in Richardson, Texas. I told him I had been by it many times when I lived in the Dallas/Ft. Worth area.

His plan was to go to the mosque during one their busiest times of prayer and to kill as many people as possible. He described all the different types of weapons he was going to use and said he would be covered with body armor from head to toe. If he had made it to the mosque he could have killed hundreds of people that day. I do not know how many people the mosque holds but it is in the hundreds. Mark said the police captured him before he could carry out his plan.

Now here is the bizarre part. This is the same mosque where the man he shot in the head worships. Of course, at this point I am beyond belief that I am standing here listening to this. I have no doubt in my mind that Mark is telling me the truth and that he would have killed all those people if he had not been stopped. Why is he telling me this? To brag about his murder spree? No. He wants me to see how God can stop something terrible from happening and then turn the situation around for His glory.

Just then, he displayed an act of unselfishness and told me that he did not want to hog my time and that other people needed to talk to me so I said good-bye.

JUNE 15, 2011

Today when I walked up to Mark's cell, he was talking to Lawrence Brewer in the next cell. Brewer is an inmate who does not care for men of God and so far will not talk to me. Mark immediately greeted me and then Brewer said, "Hey, Mark, do you know this guy?"

Mark said, "Of course. This is BroJack. It's all right to talk to him."

I thought to myself, *Mark might have just opened the door for me with this inmate for my next visit. God is good!*

I could tell Mark was more excited than usual today and I could not wait to hear why. He started telling me that he had just come back from a visit with some lawyers from London, England. They had been sent by a pen pal he had been writing to in London for over a year now. They do not have the death penalty in England so this pen pal, who happens to have a little money, sent a team of lawyers to the US to review and take over Mark's appeals. In addition, CBS anchor Scott Pelley is supposed to interview Mark on June 28th and 29th. Furthermore, the Muslim victim who survived Mark's attack is supposed to be working with the lawyers, too. Mark said that there had been more activity in the last two weeks concerning his case than in the past several years. He was so excited!

I told him that June 29th was my birthday and he asked me how old I was. I told him I quit counting after fifty.

He said, "Well, you can either tell me or I will tell CBS in the interview that you are around sixty-five."

He was laughing his head off and I said, "Go ahead, man. No one is going to believe that a good looking guy like me is sixty-five years old."

He said, "They will believe *me* because, at this point, I don't have anything to lie about. Everyone knows I'm guilty of my crimes but the question is should I be executed for them." So I whispered my age to him!

I really enjoy talking to Mark because he is one of the most for-real people I have ever met. He will tell you like it is with no reservations.

JUNE 22, 2011

Today, as soon as I got on A pod, Mark was shouting at me to come to his cell. He wanted to tell me about the dream he had just had.

Things are still happening rather fast concerning Mark's appeals but his execution date of July 20 is fast approaching as well.

Mark started telling me about his dream. He is supposed to be interviewed June 28 and 29 by CBS News and he has been worrying about what to say in an opening comment. He said that while he was asleep just now he felt like God gave him the opening line.

He said, "I am a *true*-blooded American and a *full*-blooded Christian!"

I said, "Wow! That is good! After you get through with it, I need to use it." He laughed and gave God praise for all the things that were going on. Mark had a spark of hope in his eyes. I prayed for God's will to be done in this situation.

But Mark is also a realist and he told me that he still was going to submit my name as his spiritual advisor during his execution when he filled out his fourteen-day paperwork. I did not say anything so he looked me straight in the eyes and said, "You will be there won't you?"

I said, "Only because you want me to. I am not really interested in watching you die."

"It will be all right," he said. I just smiled.

What a switch. Here is a condemned man telling me that *I* will be all right at *his* execution!

JUNE 29, 2011

Today is my birthday so it would have been very easy for me to skip my weekly visit to death row but that did not seem right, so here I am once again on the row. I had decided to cut my visit short at 5:00 p.m. so I could go to church with my sons this evening.

I did not know it but today would be the last time that I would see Mark alive. I have grown very fond of him over the last several months. One reason is because he has never once tried to blame his crime on anyone else and he has always taken full accountability for his actions. I admire him for that but what I am about to tell you will define what a true Christian is all about and, possibly, make you admire him as well.

Mark was scheduled to be executed on July 20, 2011 and he had come to accept that fact because of his faith in Jesus Christ. The Bible says you will know them by their fruits (or actions). How do I know Mark is a Christian? Because of his fruits. Despite his current circumstances, he still proclaims the name of Jesus to his fellow inmates every chance he gets and God blesses those who proclaim Him. You are probably wondering how God could bless this condemned man on death row. Let me tell you how.

Mark has an eighteen-year-old daughter he has never seen, until today! That's right; he had just come from seeing his daughter for the first time in his life and if the State of Texas has their way, it will be the last time. You would think he would be down or depressed but all he could do was give thanks to God for orchestrating the meeting; and orchestrate, He did!

Two years ago, when his daughter was sixteen, she was abducted and raped by some men in her home state of Oregon. The state had an Amber Alert out for her. The men were caught and his daughter helped the state of Oregon prosecute them. However, because of what she endured at the hands of these men, she subsequently developed a drug problem and was eventually convicted on felony drug charges. She is currently on probation.

Now this is how God works! The state of Oregon, upon hearing that her dad was about to be executed in Texas, flew her and her probation officer, at the cost of the state, to Texas so she could visit her dad before his execution. That visit just took place today! I am sometimes just blown away by the grace and mercy of God!

That is not all! After talking to his daughter, Mark told me he had just found out his mother and sister had passed away this year. After his crimes, his family had pretty much disowned him so he had not heard from anyone in years, until the news of those deaths.

Now let me sum it up for you. Here is a man on death row, scheduled to be executed in two weeks, who just heard his mother and sister are dead, and who had just finished meeting his daughter for the first and last time, and he is still giving thanks to God for being so good to him!

There is your definition of a Christian for future reference, to use when you think *you* have it rough. Now maybe you can understand why I have grown fond of Mark over the last several months. He is an inspiration to me and I will never forget him.

JULY 5, 2011

Today I received a phone call from the prison telling me that the prison is on lockdown and that I cannot get into the prison until July 29th. That is terrible news because now I will not have the opportunity to visit with Mark before his scheduled execution on July 20th. I never got to see Humberto Leal before his execution because of a lockdown and now the same thing might happen with Mark. My heart is broken; however, I have to believe that it is God's will and I must accept it. Still, it is so heartbreaking to think of Mark standing at his cell door waiting for me to visit. He had such hope in his eyes the last time we spoke. All I can do is to keep him in my prayers and pray for God's mercy on him on July 20th.

*UPDATE: MARK STROMAN - TEXAS MAN EXECUTED FOR RACE-RELATED KILLINGS

By TIMOTHY WILLIAMS

Published: July 20, 2011

A Texas man who said he wanted to kill Arabs to avenge the Sept. 11, 2001, terrorist attacks was executed on

Wednesday evening, after a last-minute appeal by one of his victims to save his life was rejected.

The man, Mark Stroman, 41, shot at least four men he mistook for Arabs in the weeks after the attacks, killing three of them. He had said he shot the men out of a sense of patriotism and likened them to acts undertaken during war.

Mr. Stroman was pronounced dead at 8:53 p.m., The Associated Press said. His surviving victim, Rais Bhuiyan, a thirty-seven-year-old immigrant from Bangladesh, who was partly blinded in his right eye after being shot in the face with a shotgun, led a campaign to spare Mr. Stroman.

On Wednesday afternoon, Lee Yeakel, a federal court judge in Austin, Texas, denied a lawsuit filed by Mr. Bhuiyan to delay the execution. Mr. Bhuiyan had sought to meet with Mr. Stroman as part of a mediation process that his and Mr. Stroman's lawyers said was guaranteed under Texas law. The lawyers tried to get a state judge to intervene, but late Wednesday the Texas Court of Criminal Appeals refused to stop the execution.

In a separate effort, Mr. Stroman's lawyers petitioned the United States Supreme Court to delay the execution because Mr. Stroman's previous legal representatives had failed to detail adequately the childhood abuse and other trouble that may have led him to go on the shooting spree. The court rejected those appeals.

In the past several months, Mr. Bhuiyan had been meeting with Texas officials and started an online petition to try to prevent the execution.

Mr. Stroman was convicted of killing Vasudev Patel, 49, an Indian immigrant, during the attempted robbery of a convenience store near Dallas in October 2001. Mr. Stroman was also charged in the fatal shooting of Waqar Hasan, 46, a Muslim born in Pakistan.

Mr. Stroman was not tried in that shooting, or that of Mr. Bhuiyan, because he had already been convicted for the murder of Mr. Patel and sentenced to death.

Mr. Stroman had a long criminal record, including time in prison for robbery and credit card fraud.

In a July 13 note posted on his blog, Mr. Stroman wrote that the last few days before his scheduled execution had been strangely rewarding.

"It is definitely an experience that has already molded me into a new person," he wrote. "I've seen so many people worldwide trying to save my life in the last few days and weeks and it's a surreal feeling. It's like my life is flashing right before my eyes. As I said in an earlier blog ... the closer I get to my death Peace I seem to find."

http://www.nytimes.com/2011/07/21/us/21death.html

HIS OFFICIAL LAST STATEMENT:

Even though I lay on this gurney, seconds away from my death, I am at total peace. May the Lord Jesus Christ be with me. I am at peace. Hate is going on in this world and it has to stop. Hate causes a lifetime of pain. Even though I lay here I am still at peace. I am still a proud American, Texas loud, Texas proud. God bless America, God bless everyone. Let's do this damn thing. Director Hazelwood, thank you very much. Thank you everyone. Spark, I love you, all of you. I love you

Conna. It's all good, it's been a great honor. I feel it; I am going to sleep now. Goodnight, 1, 2 there it goes.

BROJACK'S FINAL COMMENT:

Just like that, my friend Mark is gone. I will never forget him. The Mark I knew was a good person trying to find his purpose in life and, unfortunately, he found it too late.

Why do I think Mark committed these horrible crimes? I do not think it was just one thing but a combination of things that pushed him to make those terrible decisions. I believe that when Mark committed his crimes, he was lost. By that, I mean that he was not a born-again child of God. He committed his crimes out of a sense of *revenge*. In addition, his actions can be related to hate crimes. However, if you really get to the root you will find, like most lost people, he acted out of *ignorance*. Ignorant of the ways of God. Ignorant of the grace and mercy of God. Why do I believe that? Because only after he was saved by God did he begin to understand how wrong his actions really were. Only the Holy Spirit of God can convict us of our sins. It is impossible for us to convict ourselves without God's help.

I am thankful for one thing. I did not have to watch Mark die. Because of the lockdown, we were not able to complete the fourteen-day paperwork in time. I found out later, during my visits with another inmate, that Mark understood. Someday I will see Mark on the streets of Glory. We will remember none of this and I will give him a big Gospel hug. Amen.

Chapter 9

A Christian and a Muslim?

Do not judge, or you too will be judged. For in the same way you judge others, you will be judged, and with the measure you use, it will be measured to you.
~ Matthew 7:1-2 ~

Gayland Bradford, Inmate # 966

When we as Christians witness to someone, we need to be careful not to judge. As Matthew 7:1–2 tells us, it is not our place to judge anyone. Gayland Bradford was a professed Muslim and I am a professed Christian. Can these two beliefs meet and still respect each other? It happened with me and Gayland! As to why Gayland committed the crime of robbery and murder, let's see if my interactions and conversations with him can give us a clue.

CRIME CONVICTION: On February 22, 1990, Gayland was convicted in the shooting death of twenty-nine-year-old Brian Edward Williams during a robbery of Angelo's Food Store at 3021 M.L. King Jr. Boulevard in Dallas. Williams was shot four times with a handgun and later died of his wounds in a Dallas hospital. Bradford stole a .357 revolver, a cap, and Williams' wallet before fleeing the store. He was arrested on January 3, 1989, and later gave police a voluntary statement.

MAY 10, 2011

Because there is really no way to predict how much time I will have on the pods, I have been praying about the inmates God would like me to pursue when I get to the row. All week long as I prayed for God's guidance I keep hearing the name *Gayland Bradford*.

Gayland is a Muslim who has been on death watch for a while and has an execution date of June 1, 2011. I have not been able to talk with him in the past. He always has blinders covering the slots on each side of his cell door so no one can see into his cell. Also, the other inmates tell me he will not talk to any chaplain.

Gayland has been on death row for twenty-one years! I can't imagine that kind of existence. Day after day, month after month, year after year, locked in a 6 × 10 steel box. So, I prayed all the way to the prison today that God would supernaturally put me in front of Gayland so that I can plant just one seed.

That seed is Romans 10:9, *That if you confess with your mouth the Lord Jesus Christ, and believe in your heart that God has raised him from the dead, you will be saved.* I feel in my heart that if I can somehow get that verse to him I would fulfill my mission from God today. Don't ask me why I feel that way, I just do.

When I arrived on the row after signing in I went straight to A pod and death watch. I could not get an escort. So I went to B pod and could not get an escort. So I went to C pod and could not get an escort. Most people would have given up at this point but I am not most people.

While waiting on an escort, I decided I would do something different and just stand outside of the control booth for a while in hopes of getting a feeling of what it might be like to live under these conditions for years and years. I'd done this once before but wanted to try it again.

At first there was a lot of noise from inmates shouting and from doors opening and closing. All doors are opened electronically from the control booth. A red light shines at each section when a cell door is open.

After about ten minutes, it got very quiet and it was then I got a glimpse of the loneliness and emptiness that exists in this place. I had feelings of hopelessness, discouragement, terror, and many other emotions that I cannot describe. This is a place where no one should end up but it is also a place that society needs. As I was standing there, I started thinking about the millions of kids who are caught up in illegal activities that could land them in this place. They have no idea what awaits them. I had an overwhelming conviction that I somehow needed to tell these kids about this place and maybe they will change their course. I did not know it but it was at this very moment that God had given me my next assignment. To take what He has shown me in this place to His children. After about twenty minutes, I could not take any more. I told the guard that I would try another pod.

Now whoever is reading this is about to experience the activity of God. You are about to see how God can open a door when no one else can. I was buzzed into A pod and the guard at the control booth said she had a guard who could escort me but for only about fifteen minutes. I said I'd take it. I headed straight for Gayland's cell but as usual, he had his openings covered up.

Needless to say, I was disappointed but I could not let my feelings show because almost immediately Mark Stroman, who was in the cell beside him, came to his door and we started talking.

Now it was time for God to open doors. As I was talking to Mark, the guard who was escorting me must have overheard me telling Mark that I was hoping to talk to Gayland, so he shouted through Gayland's cell door. To my surprise down came the covers over Gayland's openings.

In the blink of an eye, I found myself face-to-face with Gayland Bradford. I had been trying to meet this inmate for weeks and now it was finally happening! I introduced myself quickly as BroJack and asked if he would mind talking with me. He knew that I was there representing Jesus Christ and to my surprise he said okay.

Just then Mark, sensing what was about to happen, called the guard to his cell to occupy him and now I was all alone with Gayland. I think I stumbled around for a little bit and felt like kicking myself in the rear for not being better prepared. But then I could feel God taking over and the conversation started to smooth out.

I found that Gayland was very soft-spoken and at times it was difficult understanding what he was saying. I tried to let him do all the talking but in the back of mind, I kept hearing Romans 10:9. How was I going to get this message to him? Then I saw my opening. He asked if I was a Christian and I replied yes. I asked him if he was a Muslim and he said yes. For some reason, we both just smiled at each other. There was a brief moment of silence and then big mouth me asked him a question.

I said, "Gayland, as a Muslim, is there anything you would like to ask me as a Christian?"

He said, "I can't think of anything right now."

Then I said, "Well, then as a Christian, can I ask you something?" To my relief he said sure. I asked, "I know you have a copy of the Koran but by chance do you have a copy of the Christian Bible?" He went over to a shelf in his cell and retrieved a copy of the Holy Bible. I then said, "I am not here to debate religions but I would like to ask you a kind favor. Would you mind reading Romans 10:9 when you get a chance? God has put that verse on my heart to give to you and I have to be obedient to His will."

He smiled and said he would. I was so happy I could have shouted at the top of my lungs...*Hallelujah! Hallelujah!*

I ended our meeting by thanking him for talking to me. I told him I knew he had a choice and I thanked him for choosing to speak with me. He said that, if I wanted to, I could stop by his cell on my next visit and my heart almost jumped out of my chest as I said sure.

My time was up and I smiled at Mark as I was escorted from A pod. We both knew that God had just orchestrated my meeting with Gayland, but that God had also used Mark to occupy the guard. What an awesome God we serve!

MAY 17, 2011

Today as I approached Gayland's cell, he was sitting at his little desk with headphones on, writing a letter. As he looked up he could not see me very well because he didn't have his glasses on. I fully expected him to say he was busy writing letters but he didn't. He put on his glasses and when he saw it was me a big smile came over his face and he stopped what was doing and came to his cell door so we could talk.

My heart was pumping so fast I could feel it through my shirt. I asked how he was doing and he said okay. We had some small talk for a few minutes then I got right to it. I said, "Did you get a chance to read that verse I gave you last week?" I'd given him Romans 10:9 to read.

He smiled and said, "Yes, I did." Man I was really getting excited at this point.

Then for some reason, I said, "Gayland, has anyone else given you that verse to read?" A serious look came over his face and he said, "I haven't really talked to anybody else."

I said, "You mean no other chaplains have come to see you?"

He said, "No, there have been plenty of chaplains, preachers, and prison counselors come by but they just ask how I am and quickly move on."

I asked, "Why don't you talk to them?"

What he said next broke my heart. "I would have liked to talk to some of them but they were all too afraid."

I said, "Afraid of what?"

"Afraid of me," he said meekly. I asked him how he knew that. He said, "I could see it in their eyes. They all had fear in their eyes."

I was perplexed for a minute because here we were talking like two old friends and I just met him two weeks ago. I asked him, "Well, what about me? You're talking to me?"

He looked at me as serious as anyone ever has and said, "I don't see any fear in your eyes. I feel like you are genuinely concerned about me and you are not judging me."

I immediately said, "That's because I walk in here with God's protection and I will walk out of here with His protection. No one can take me out of this world except God and when that time comes there is nothing I can do about it anyway. And as for judging you, that is not for me to do. That is God's responsibility not mine."

He smiled. I felt like we understood each other and it seemed like we had been friends for a long time. I told him that I would come back next Tuesday and if he wanted to talk, I would come by.

He said, "I hope you do."

MAY 24, 2011

Today as I was making my way to A pod, my heart was pounding. I wanted so desperately to present the Gospel to Gayland. He saw me coming and got up and came to his door; so far, so good.

I knew because his execution was fast approaching that he would be doing all the visiting with family members he could at this point so I asked how his visits went and he said they were great! I asked if he had heard from the courts because they were supposed to rule on his appeal last Thursday. He said that they decided to proceed with his execution. I was stunned for a moment because — what do you say to a guy who just told you that he will be executed next Wednesday. He has a little over a week to live! He could tell I was shaken so he told me that it would be all right. Again, here was a condemned man consoling me instead of the other way around!

I didn't know if it was the proper time but I asked him if he would allow me to do something for him. He asked what and I said, "Gayland, I wonder if you would indulge me by letting me present the Gospel of Jesus Christ to you. You are under no obligation and I fully understand if you say no. I respect your wishes."

He looked at me for a minute and then said, "Sure." I was so excited I felt like I was going to faint but I had to keep my composure because this could possibly be the most important time of Gayland Bradford's life.

It took me about ten minutes to take him down the Romans Road and to explain how that all have sinned and that because of that sin we would be separated from God for eternity. I then explained that because God knew that and because He loves us so, He sacrificed His Son Jesus so we could be saved. I then told Gayland he too could be saved and then I told him how. He listened to every word. He was very patient with me and I feel in my heart that he heard what God had to say. Man, if I could have given him a hug I would have.

I thanked him from the bottom of my heart for allowing me to do this. He smiled and said, "You are welcome, BroJack."

I told him I would come back next Tuesday to see him one more time and he seemed happy to hear that. I prayed with him and said good-bye. Once again, my time on the row was over. As usual I just shook my head in disbelief as I headed to the main gate and freedom. Amen?

MAY 31, 2011

Today, when I got to Gayland's cell, he was smiling.

He said, "I have two hours in the dayroom and it would probably be better if we talked there."

I said sure and Gayland asked the guard if he could start his dayroom time. The guard approved and within minutes, Gayland was in the dayroom and we were face-to-face. The dayroom is like a traditional jail cell with black bars and it is centered so that all the cells surround it. If inmates are on good behavior then they are allowed to come out of their cells into the dayroom. Only one at a time though. It is easier to talk to an inmate through those bars instead of the small opening on the side of their cell door. You have to be very careful during this time though. If you get too close, an inmate can grab you and possibly break your neck before someone could rescue you. I am always on high alert during these times.

I immediately asked him about his appeal last Thursday and he said it was all over. They had upheld the decision to execute him and he would die the next day. I panicked for a moment because I did not really know what to say. I mean, really, what do you say to someone who has just told you that he will die tomorrow?

I tried to change the subject by asking how his visit went. He said he got to spend most of the day with his mother and daughter. I panicked again! I could not imagine telling my sons good-bye, knowing I would be

144

put to death the next day. Gayland said that he was predicting to his daughter that he would be pronounced dead at exactly 6:08 p.m. tomorrow evening. He was laughing about it!

We had an awkward moment of silence and then I just blurted out, "So tomorrow you go to heaven to be with God, right? There is no doubt in your mind, right?"

He smiled at me and said, "I am going home. Come on, man. I have been here for twenty-one years. I am tired of living like this. Twenty-one years is enough! Could you handle this?"

I said, "I could not handle it for twenty-one hours."

He said, "Then everything will be all right. I am ready to go."

I started feeling a little better about his situation. He was okay so I should be all right also but I had a sick feeling in my stomach. We joked about him getting to heaven before me and I said, "You don't know that for sure. I could get killed on the way home tonight!"

He smiled and said, "God is not through with you yet. You're not getting out of here that easy."

I smiled too, and said, "I hear you."

Then with a great big lump in my throat, I said, "Gayland, I want you to know that you have blessed my life these last few weeks. I will never forget you and your testimony will live on through me as I preach to people around the world. When I get to heaven someday, we will know each other. We will not know how we know each other only that we do. Until that day, I will miss you."

He said, "It will be all right."

I looked him straight in the eye and said, "I love you, brother."

He replied, "I love you too, man."

I turned and left A pod knowing that, barring some miracle tomorrow, I would never see Gayland again on this Earth.

145

*UPDATE: GAYLAND BRADFORD
WED JUNE 1, 2011, 7:45 P.M. EDT

Texas, on Wednesday, June 1, 2011, executed a man who shot and killed a security guard during a 1988 robbery at a Dallas grocery store.

Gayland Bradford, 42, was the fourth person executed in Texas this year and the second put to death using a new drug, pentobarbital, which is often used to euthanize animals.

Bradford died at 6:25 p.m. local time, nine minutes after the drug was administered, said Jason Clark, spokesman for the Texas Department of Criminal Justice.

On December 28, 1988, Bradford told his girlfriend he was going to make some money, showing her a gun before he left her apartment with two other people, according to a report by the Texas attorney general's office.

Later that night, he went to a grocery store and shot store security guard Brian Williams in the back. Bradford then took the guard's gun and shot him repeatedly while he was on the ground, according to the report.

Bradford told an accomplice to take Williams' money, which turned out to be only seven dollars. The accomplice also took personal items from Williams, including his hat and pipe. Williams died about an hour later, the report said.

According to the report, Bradford and the accomplice left without taking anything else. The store's security camera recorded the events and Bradford later confessed he went to the store to "get some money," and that he shot the guard, the report said.

Before his death, Bradford said he was at peace and that he had no worries.

"Victim's family, may you be at peace also," he said.

Bradford's last meal was chicken with jalapenos, peanut butter cake, butter rolls, two steak and cheese omelets, hash browns and ketchup, and a root beer soda.

Bradford's execution was the 20th in the United States this year. There are three more executions scheduled this month in Texas, where more than four times as many people have been executed as any other state since the death penalty was reinstated in the United States in 1976, according to the Death Penalty Information Center.

HIS OFFICIAL LAST STATEMENT:

Noel, I love you man. You have been there for me through thick and thin, you and Brigitta. Be there for each other. I am at peace, we have no worries, just as I have no more worries. To the victim's family, may you be at peace also.

BROJACK'S FINAL COMMENTS:

I will miss Gayland and our conversations. It is amazing how quickly you can get to know someone and how quickly they can be gone; never to be seen on this Earth again. My heart is sad for the families of both Gayland and the victim of his crime. Everyone loses in this situation. I take comfort in knowing that Gayland allowed me to present the Gospel of Jesus Christ to him and only God and Gayland know for sure if he listened and surrendered his life to Jesus. This story is proof that two men can meet and respect each other's religious beliefs and still treat one another with respect. Amen!

Why did Gayland commit this crime of murder? *Robbery* was the primary reason. Many of the inmates on the row have the same circumstances surrounding their crimes. They started out to commit what they considered a simple robbery for whatever reason and it escalated to murder.

147

In Gayland's case, he became a product of his environment, which led him to a life of violence. However, there has to be more to it. There has to be something other than just a bad neighborhood that influences a person to kill. We will never know Gayland's real motive. Only he and God know for sure why he really killed another human being. *Why* is not important now though. Did he listen as I presented the Gospel of Jesus Christ to him? The answer to this question is all that matters now!

Chapter 10

Alcohol, Drugs, and Premature Death

Be sober minded; be watchful. Your adversary the devil prowls around like a roaring lion, seeking someone to devour.

~ 1 Peter 5:8 ~

Milton Mathis, Inmate #999337

There are things that we allow in our lives that will lead us to premature death. At the time, we may not recognize how harmful some of these things are until it is too late. Such was the case of Milton Mathis.

CRIME CONVICTION: On December 15, 1998, at approximately 8:30 a.m., Mathis shot three victims in the head with a .45 caliber pistol at a known drug house in Ft. Bend County, Texas. One of the victims, a fifteen-year old Hispanic female survived the shooting, paralyzed from the chest down. Mathis reportedly turned the gun on two other intended victims, however, when he attempted to pull the trigger, the gun either misfired or had been jammed.

APRIL 5, 2011

Today I met Milton Mathis for the first time. I was on C pod visiting some other inmates when the opportunity came for me to meet him. He immediately wanted to know if I was a state chaplain and I said, "No, I am a volunteer chaplain."

Then he asked me something interesting. He said, "Why would you come in here to tell people about Jesus when a lot of the inmates could care less."

I simply replied, "If I am a Christian, then how could I not."

I believe he understood and respected my answer because he then told me that he was supposed to get an execution date soon and he hoped he got to see me again. I told him that if he got a date I would find him on A pod and I thanked him for talking to me. Even though this was a brief encounter, I felt as though we would be talking more in the near future.

MAY 17, 2011

Today, as I was going from cell to cell on A pod I found myself face-to-face with Milton Mathis. I had a brief encounter with him on April 5th on C pod and he told me at that time that he was close to getting an execution date. I told him when he got one I would see him on A pod deathwatch. And sure enough, there he was.

He immediately remembered me and said, "I told you I was about to get a date and here I am." I asked how he was doing and he replied okay. I listened to some small talk for a while and I then I brought Jesus into the conversation.

I boldly asked him, "Have you come to a spiritual place in your life where you know for certain that if you were to die today that you would go to heaven, or is that something you would say that you are still working on?"

He didn't think long about it and he replied, "I am positive I am going to heaven."

So I said, "How can you be sure?"

He replied, "Because I have given my life to Jesus Christ and I belong to Him."

I said, "Good answer, Milton."

I saw a surprised look on his face and he said, "What did you just say?"

I thought to myself, *What did I say?* Did I just say something stupid, which I am very good at by the way. I replied, "I just said good answer."

He responded, "No, you called me by my name. I can't believe you remembered my name. You can't imagine the people who come through here and talk to me for a little while and never even ask my name. And yet it has been almost two months since we briefly talked and you remembered my name!"

I said, "Well, I have to give God all the glory because I forget my own name sometimes." He laughed and thanked me again for remembering his name. To me that was not such a big thing but to him it was monumental. I felt like I had gained a friend for life.

Milton was scheduled to be executed on June 21, 2011, which was a little over a month away. I thanked him for talking to me and told him I needed to try to talk to Gayland Bradford, whose execution was very soon, before I lost my escort. He understood and I moved on.

JUNE 7, 2011

I have not been able to talk with Milton since last month, for various reasons. One time he was out in visitation. One time his pod was on lockdown. I have learned that you cannot count on seeing someone in

151

this place on a regular basis so I have begun to treat every encounter like it will be the last time I see that person.

Milton had eleven days to live if they executed him on June 21. He had everything in his cell divided up into groups. He was getting his belongings together to give away, either to other inmates or various family members. He told me he had been completing his fourteen-day paper work all day for his upcoming execution.

I asked how he was doing and he said good considering the circumstances. I don't think he was feeling sorry for himself because he had expressed to me that he was ready to pay for his crimes.

"Living like this in a steel cage is not living," he said.

I had to ask, "So, in a little over a week from now, when you leave this Earth, you know without a doubt where you are headed."

He smiled and said, "Without a doubt." He said that, lately, he had been asking God over and over again to forgive him and I told him, "Milton, you only have to ask God once to forgive you of a particular sin and He is faithful and just to do so. You don't need to keep bringing it up because God has already cast it away, as far as the east is from the west. He has already forgotten about it." Milton seemed happy with that statement and I asked if I could pray with him. He immediately bowed his head and moved closer.

After our prayer together, I thanked him and said, "If I don't get to see you again on this Earth, I will see you on the streets of Glory."

He smiled and said, "You know that's right!" He stuck his finger through the wire-mesh screen and I grabbed it and said, "I love you brother."

He replied, "I love you too, BroJack."

JUNE 15, 2011

Today I went up to the second tier to Milton's cell and thank God he was waiting for me. He was smiling and he said, "I was hoping you would come and see me. I heard you on the pod." He said, "Guess who is coming to see me in person this Thursday and Friday?" Before I could answer, he said, "My mother! They would not allow me to see her in person ever since her and my sister came to see me six months ago and they found a marijuana seed in their car. My mom and sister do not even smoke pot but my sister's boyfriend at the time did. Anyway, I have not been allowed to see my mom in over six months."

Every time he spoke about his mother, his face would light up like a ten-year-old boy. I could tell this man loved his mother. I told him I was very happy for him. I know Milton is ready to meet God face to face but I could still tell by some of his comments that he would rather stay on Earth with his mother, even if it meant being locked up.

One of the things I admire about Milton is that he has always taken accountability for his crimes. He told me on numerous occasions that he is guilty of his crimes and that he should be punished. What he doesn't agree with is the statement from the state that says he cannot be rehabilitated. He believes in his heart that God has changed him, especially during these last six years on death row.

He was scheduled to be executed six years ago but got a stay of execution. For these last six years, he feels he has become a new person in Jesus Christ. Milton just kept talking and I just kept listening. I didn't have any more advice and I knew right now he just needed someone who would listen.

When I saw that he was finished, I asked if I could pray with him and he agreed. I was thinking to myself this might be the last time I have to pray with this man on Earth so I wanted to say the right things. These farewell prayers are starting to take their toll on me but I have to continue until God says otherwise.

After our prayer, I shook Milton's finger as he stuck it through the wire mesh and said, "God bless you, brother. I love you man."

He said, "I love you too, BroJack." I don't know if Milton will be here when I come back next week. I have such an empty feeling inside of me when I think about it.

It was time for me to leave the row and go home. I pray that God was able to use me to help someone in this place today. I pray that my visit has not been in vain. To God be the glory!

*UPDATE: MILTON MATHIS, TUESDAY, JUNE 21, 2011 8:51 P.M. EDT

(Reuters) — Texas executed on Tuesday a man convicted of fatally shooting two people and paralyzing a third near Houston in 1998, despite evidence that he was mentally disabled.

Milton Mathis, 32, was sentenced in 1999, before the U.S. Supreme Court ruled it unconstitutional to execute inmates with mental disabilities. His supporters had been trying for years to argue that he should be spared.

On Tuesday, a final plea to the Supreme Court to hear evidence of his mental disability was denied, and he was executed by lethal injection.

He was pronounced dead at 6:53 p.m. local time, said Jason Clark, a Texas Department of Criminal Justice spokesman.

Mathis was the 23rd person executed in the United States this year and the sixth executed in Texas, the most active death penalty state in the nation.

Shortly before he died, Mathis criticized the Texas death penalty as a "mass slaughter."

"The system has failed me. This is a miscarriage of justice," he said.

Turning to Melanie Almaguer, who had been paralyzed from the neck down since the shooting, and who witnessed the execution, he said that he "never meant" to hurt her, according to Clark.

"You were just in the wrong place at the wrong time," Mathis said.

His last meal included two burgers with bacon, fried pork chops, fried chicken, fried fish, chili cheese fries, regular fries, and fruit punch, Clark said.

HIS OFFICIAL LAST STATEMENT:

Yes, sir. I just want to say to all my supporters, family, and friends: I love ya'll and appreciate ya'll. To the ones representing me today, thank you for everything. The system has failed me. This is a miscarriage of justice. There are people on death row that need help. I love my family. I love you, too, Mom. I am all right. I asked the Lord to have mercy on me and I hope He has mercy on these people carrying out this mass slaughter. They have no respect for humanity.

To Melanie, I never meant to hurt you. You were just in the wrong place at the wrong time. I am not asking for your forgiveness. All I have to worry about is God forgiving me. I hope you get better and for the doctors to continue to take care of you. Take care of my mother for me. To everybody, know that I love you and I am okay. Lord, have mercy on my soul. Lord, have mercy on my soul. Lord, have mercy on these peoples' soul. Life is not supposed to end this way. No more pain and frustration. When I knock at the gates, they will open up and let me in. To my mom and everybody, I love you. I can feel it right now. My life, my life.

BROJACK'S FINAL COMMENTS:

Milton has touched my heart with his loyalty and obedience to God. I keep thinking about how much he loved his mother who surely misses him very much. What a tragedy and what a waste.

Why did Milton murder two people and cripple another? Milton, like millions of others in this world, did not weigh the cost of his involvement with alcohol and drugs, particularly with drugs. He committed his crimes in a known drug house and, by his own admission, under the influence of drugs. Would he have done what he did if he was not there or under the influence of drugs? The percentages go way down when you delete those two circumstances.

One of the most dangerous things that most people do not take in consideration when doing drugs is the people or places you have to associate with in order to get the drugs. Case in point: fifteen-year-old Melanie Almaguer. She was in the drug house when Milton went on his killing spree. He shot her in the head. She survived but today she is paralyzed from the neck down. Was she in the wrong place at the wrong time? You bet she was! Would she have been there if it were not for the drugs? Probably not. The Bible says in 1 Corinthians 15:33, *Do not be misled: Bad company corrupts good character."* Not only do you risk your life when you take drugs, you also risk your life trying to acquire them.

Milton became a murderer and lost his life prematurely because of drugs. I believe drugs and alcohol are a very powerful weapon satan uses against us. There are so many things he can get us to do once we are under the influence. Be careful!

I didn't know Milton when he committed his crimes but I did know him before he was executed and what I saw was a God-fearing man. God bless you, brother.

Chapter 11

Peace in Death

And the peace of God, which transcends all understanding, will guard
your hearts and your minds in Christ Jesus.
~ Philippians 4:7 ~

Lawrence Brewer, Inmate # 999327

Since I started my visits to death row, at this point ten men who I knew very well have been executed. As their time of execution drew near, it was evident who belonged to God and who did not. Those who belonged to God had a peace that transcends all understanding. Those who did not were defiant to the end. As I got to know Brewer (as he was called on the row), I felt like he wanted to trust in God and have the peace that can only come from Him, but he seemed to carry a giant steel chain of anger around his neck that eventually choked the very life from his body. He came close to accepting God. I wonder how close?

CRIME CONVICTION: Brewer was convicted in the murder of a black male occurring on June 7, 1998. The offense involved Brewer and two codefendants torturing and killing a forty-nine-year old handicapped black male during the nighttime hours, in rural Jasper County, Texas. The victim was observed in the back of a pickup truck occupied by Brewer and his codefendants. This was the last occasion the victim was seen alive by persons other than Brewer and his codefendants. Brewer and his codefendants drove to an isolated spot on a logging road where they beat and tormented the victim, then tied him to a logging chain, which was hooked to the pickup truck. Brewer and his codefendants then dragged the victim to his death, leaving his decapitated and dismembered body to be found the following day by citizens and law enforcement officials. It was argued in court that Brewer and his codefendants engaged in this criminal act, in part, due to their racially separatist affiliation with the Confederate Knights of America and the Ku Klux Klan. Brewer and one codefendant were documented members of the Confederate Knights of America and a large amount of Ku Klux Klan and other racial separatist organizations' paraphernalia was discovered in a residence occupied by the three.

JUNE 15, 2011

Today I met Lawrence Brewer for the first time. I did not know it yet but this was going to be a real stormy relationship. While standing in front of his cell door, I introduced myself as a volunteer chaplain and asked if he felt like talking. He immediately said no. I thanked him anyway and told him I would be on the pod for a while and if he changed his mind, I would be happy to come back. I did not have high hopes that Lawrence would talk to me anytime soon but I have to keep trying.

JUNE 29, 2011

Today I started to Lawrence Brewer's cell because it is the first one to the left on the first tier. I figured I would start on the lower left, work my way to the right, move to the second tier and do the same thing. Brewer was on his bed reading as I came to his cell door.

He did not move so I quickly realized he was not interested in talking to me. It did not stop me though from asking how he was doing and this time he stopped reading and said, "I am okay considering my circumstances." I asked if he would like to talk about them and he said no. I told him if he changed his mind to call for me and I would come back. He said okay. I feel like he is getting more comfortable with me but I am not sure. I am praying that God will show me a way to get through to him.

JULY 27, 2011

It has been three weeks since I have been able to visit death row because of lockdowns. Today when I got to A pod, I headed straight for Brewer's cell. I have been trying to get him to talk to me for weeks but with little success. Today was different. Mark Stroman, who was in the cell next to him, had been executed last week and I think that affected everyone on the row.

I spoke to Brewer and asked how he was doing and he said fine. However, this time he stopped what he was doing and actually came over to his cell door to talk. I told him it had been weeks since I had been able to come inside and to my surprise, he said he knew and understood.

He said Mark wanted me to know that he understood why I could not be there in his final hours and to tell me he will be waiting for me on the streets of Glory. I could feel my emotions welling up inside but I tried to control them as much as I could. I was so thankful that Mark understood why I could not be there for his execution. Brewer did not know it but he just gave me some great relief.

Then he began to talk about how he noticed that Humberto Leal and Mark both had this unusual peace about them even up to the day they were taken away to be executed. I smiled and said, "I know exactly where that peace comes from. It comes from having assurance that when you leave this world you know that you will be with God in heaven. I have that same peace and anyone who has accepted God's free gift of salvation can also have it."

I could tell Brewer was listening but I could also tell if I pushed more, he would back off. So I said, "I cannot get that peace for you but I can tell you how you can get it."

He smiled and said, "I need to get saved, huh?"

I smiled back and said, "Exactly."

There was a brief moment of silence and then I said, "If you come to a point that you want to know how you can have that peace and assurance, I will be glad to present the Gospel of Jesus Christ to you and then you can take it from there."

He said, "I appreciate it, BroJack."

I responded, "I appreciate you talking to me. I will be back next week and I will come to your cell first."

He said, "Okay, man."

Then I got really brave. I asked if I could pray with him and he said okay. I prayed briefly for God to show him how he could have peace even in his current situation. *Man, I was excited!* I am not exactly sure but I do not think Brewer had ever talked to a preacher or minister before. Once again, God had opened another door and now I was feeling a little ashamed because I had been thinking about not coming back. What a mistake *that* would have been. I thanked God for using Brewer to straighten me out.

AUGUST 10, 2011

Today as I approached Brewer's cell, he was in his bed reading but I interrupted him anyway. I asked how he was doing and he said fine. He asked if John King, his partner in his crime, had any information about a lawyer for him. I told him he did not have the name of a lawyer but that he recommends he contact somebody at an organization called "The

Innocence Project of Texas". I did not say anything but I do not think there is any doubt that Brewer and John King are guilty. I think they are fighting the death sentence. Either way, I do not get involved in their cases.

Then I felt God giving me some direction and I said, "Hey, man, I want to give you something to think about over the next week. I want you to think about letting me present the Gospel of Jesus Christ to you. It will not hurt and it will not take long. After I am finished, you can do with it what you want. Because the bottom line is this, only you can save yourself. I can tell you why you need to be saved and how you can be saved, but it is ultimately between you and God, not me, you, and God. Would you think about it?"

He said, "I will, BroJack."

I said, "Okay, then. I'll leave you alone unless you want to talk about something else."

He said, "No, thanks." So I moved on to the next inmate.

AUGUST 17, 2011

Today I am very excited because I might get a chance to witness to Brewer about Jesus. As I came up to his cell, he had just woken up. I asked how he was doing and I could tell he was very agitated. He gave me a quick reply of, "All right I guess." At this point, I should have realized that he was bothered by my presence but for some reason it did not register with me. Then I said it. I said the very thing that sent him over the edge. I asked if he remembered our conversation last week about possibly letting me present the Gospel to him.

Then he let me have it! He started pacing back and forth in his small cell and complaining that every time he turned around some bleeping chaplain was trying to tell him about God.

Every time he took a step, he cussed more and louder. Finally, I apologized, said okay, and moved to the next cell. Now here is where some pastors would have left or took it personally. The majority of pastors are not used to being talked to that way because of their position. They are usually surrounded by Christians in a church setting where someone might occasionally get out of line but never to this extent. They are used to praise from their church members and sometimes become prideful and may not even know it. It takes a reality check like this sometimes to bring them back to the real world.

I realized a long time ago that it is not personal. These inmates do not know me personally so when they lash out it is not at *me*; it is at what I represent. I represent Jesus Christ, not BroJack. It is still hard to take sometimes though. Your defensive mode wants to kick in but I have learned that the moment you let your emotions take over is the moment you lose your witness. So, when I find myself in a situation like this, I immediately remove myself. Next week if I get the chance, I will apologize again for catching him at a bad time but not for wanting to present the Gospel to him. For that, I will never apologize!

AUGUST 24, 2011

Today as I entered A pod on death row I was trying to decide whether to try to visit with Brewer or not, considering our last encounter. He is not a big fan of what I represent, however, being a representative of God I had to try.

So, as I approached his cell I said, "Hey, Brewer! How are you today?"

He was on his bed reading. He looked up and smiled, "I'm doing good."

I replied, "Well, alrighty then." I did not pursue it any farther. I cannot make someone listen to the Gospel. I can only look for opportunities. He had four weeks to live if the State of Texas had their way. He needed to talk to someone about Jesus!

AUGUST 31, 2011

For some reason, my heart was very heavy today as I got ready to enter the prison. I did not know why but as usual, I had to pray and suck it up before I enter death row because I did not want the inmates to notice any problems I might be going through. My problems are minor compared to what these guys are facing. Therefore, I put on my happy face and entered the prison.

After I made it to the row, while I was talking to another death-row inmate, Brewer was asking who was out there, so I went to his cell door to say hello. Remember that he has not always been happy to see me. However, I cannot let that stop me from trying because on September 21, 2011, three weeks from today, the State of Texas plans to execute him. I am sure he does not understand the urgency of his situation when it comes to his salvation. I only have two more opportunities after today and I hope his heart softens enough for the Gospel of Jesus Christ to enter.

I went to his cell and replied, "It's BroJack."

He said, "Awe, okay." I could tell by his reply he was not interested in talking to me but I had to try.

I knew I was risking another cussing out but I said, "Anything you would like to talk about today?"

He smiled at me and said, "No, not today."

I feel so bad for him because if he leaves this world not knowing Jesus Christ as his Savior, the life he has spent on death row will be a cakewalk compared to eternity spent separated from God. My heart is hurting for him. However, I had no choice but to say good-bye and move on. You cannot force someone to listen to the Gospel. God gave us free will and that free will can lead us to either eternal glory with God or eternal damnation with satan. It is our choice, not God's.

SEPTEMBER 7, 2011

Today, just for the heck of it, I looked into Brewer's cell and said hello. He was laying in his bed as usual reading a book and listening to his IPod. He did take time to stop and say hello. I asked if he wanted to talk and he said no but he smiled this time. I told him I would be on the pod for a while and, if he changed his mind, just give me a shout. He smiled and said okay.

I am so sad for this man. I know he committed a horrible act of murder but as an ambassador of Jesus Christ, I have to lay those things aside and try to deliver the message of Jesus to him. I will continue to pray as his execution day quickly approaches.

SEPTEMBER 14, 2011

Today, before I went to A pod, I first visited John King on B pod, who was one of Brewer's codefendants. I have been talking to John for months now and, unlike his counterpart, he is soaking up the Word of God. John gave me a message of hope to deliver to Brewer and I said I would.

As I was approaching Brewer's cell, I thought about the message that John King wanted me to deliver. Surely, Brewer would listen to that whether he wanted to talk to me or not. I was wrong. I looked into his cell and he was in his bed with the covers over his head. Normally I would not wake an inmate if they were sleeping but I was running out of time and so was Brewer. So I shouted loud enough for him to hear but he never moved. I continued with the message from John just as though he were hearing it. I am not sure but I have an underlying suspicion that he heard every word I said. I hope so.

At this point, I have no idea if Brewer is saved and my heart is broken for him. He has no idea what he is facing. Being executed next week is one thing but spending eternity separated from God is an unbearable thought. I pray that he does not leave this world without Jesus as his Lord and Savior. I felt that I did the best I could for Brewer but I still am very concerned for him.

*UPDATE: LAWRENCE BREWER

SEPTEMBER 21, 2011. LAWRENCE BREWER, CONVICTED IN JASPER DRAGGING DEATH, HAS BEEN EXECUTED

Jasper, Texas (KTRE) — One of three suspects in one of the most grisly hate crime murders in recent Texas history has himself been put to death.

Appeals to the courts for 44-year-old Lawrence Russell Brewer were exhausted and no last-day attempts were filed to keep him from execution after 6:00 Wednesday evening in Huntsville.

Brewer requested an extensive last meal that included two chicken fried steaks, a triple-meat bacon cheeseburger, fried okra, a pound of barbecue, and a pint of ice cream.

It has been 13 years since the nation learned of the brutal dragging death of James Byrd, Jr., a black man chained to the back of a pickup truck and dragged along Huff Creek Road in Jasper to his death.

Brewer, a purported white supremacist, was condemned for fastening 49-year-old James Byrd, Jr., to the truck on June 7, 1998. Byrd's decapitated body, first thought to be animal road kill, was found the next day. Witnesses told investigators they saw Byrd walking on a road not far from his home in Jasper during the early morning hours of June 7. Byrd lived off disability checks.

He did not have a car and walked where he needed to go. Another witness saw Byrd in the bed of a pickup truck.

Testimony during the trial indicated Brewer, John King, and Sean Berry drove out into the county about 10 miles and stopped along the rural road. A fight started, ending with Byrd being tied to the truck bumper with a 24 ½ foot logging chain. Evidence indicated Byrd was dragged for three miles, then dumped near a church and cemetery, his remains leaving a bloody trail. Investigators identified Byrd's body from fingerprints taken from the headless torso.

Prior to Byrd's murder, Brewer had served a prison sentence for drug possession and burglary.

"Today is a good day as well as a sad day and what I mean by that is that I'm okay because I have gotten peace with everything and the sad thing about it is that he says he has no remorse and that saddens me," said Betty Boatner, Byrd's sister.

Boatner still lives in Jasper and says she often visits her brother's grave. She says even though their parents taught them about forgiveness it was a still a process for them to forgive their brother's killer. "We forgave him. We didn't convict him."

"I don't want him to die because it's easy. All he's going to do is go to sleep. My father didn't have that choice to go to sleep," said Renee Mullins, Byrd's daughter. Byrd's son also spoke out against the execution. Two of Byrd's sisters planned to attend Wednesday's execution. Byrd's mother, Stella, died last year.

The horrific murder of Byrd set into motion a call for special hate crime laws in Texas. It later led to the Federal October 22, 2009 Matthew Shepard and James Byrd, Jr., Hate Crimes Prevention Act, commonly known as the Matthew Shepard Act. President Barack Obama signed the bill into law on October 28, 2009.

There were two others convicted in Byrd's murder. John King is serving a death-row sentence in Polk County. His case is still under appeal and no execution date has been set. Sean Berry is serving a life sentence in Brazoria County.

The racism stigma lingers in the small town, some say, pointing to a recent attempt to oust three black city council members who helped confirm a black man as police chief. Many others say the label is unfair.

http://www.ktre.com/story/15519223/man-convicted-in-jasper-dragging-death-executed

*UPDATE: SEPTEMBER 23, 2011

Michael Graczyk, Associated Press

Houston (Associated Press) — Texas inmates who are set to be executed will no longer get their choice of last meals, a change prison officials made Thursday after a prominent state senator became miffed over an expansive request from a man condemned for a notorious dragging death.

Lawrence Russell Brewer, who was executed Wednesday for the hate crime slaying of James Byrd, Jr., more than a decade ago, asked for two chicken fried steaks, a triple-meat bacon cheeseburger, fried okra, a pound of

167

barbecue, three fajitas, a meat lover's pizza, a pint of ice cream, and a slab of peanut butter fudge with crushed peanuts. Prison officials said Brewer did not eat any of it.

"It is extremely inappropriate to give a person sentenced to death such a privilege," Senator John Whitmire, chairman of the Senate Criminal Justice Committee, wrote in a letter Thursday to Brad Livingston, the executive director of the Texas Department of Criminal Justice.

Within hours, Livingston said the senator's concerns were valid and the practice of allowing death-row offenders to choose their final meal was history.

"Effective immediately, no such accommodations will be made," Livingston said. "They will receive the same meal served to other offenders on the unit."

That had been the suggestion from Whitmire, who called the traditional request "ridiculous."
http://www.huffingtonpost.com/2011/09/22/special-last-meals-texas-_n_976543.html?icid=maing grid7%7Cmain5%7Cdl1%7Csec1_lnk3%7C98288

HIS OFFICIAL LAST STATEMENT:

No, I have no final statement.

BROJACK'S FINAL COMMENT:

It appears Brewer was defiant to the end. My heart aches for him because, if he did not accept God's gift of salvation, he is in a far worse place than death row in Texas. What a tragedy! However, I do not believe that Brewer was as mean as he would like people to think. I believe he was more afraid of death than he was anything else. Fear makes you act in strange ways sometimes. It is my prayer that in the quiet moments lying in his cell at night that somehow the Holy Spirit of God was able to convict him of his sins and through the Holy Spirit Brewer received God's gift of salvation.

As to why he committed this crime, I am not sure. The world called it a hate crime because the victim was black and the offenders were all white. I have never really understood racism because, in reality, there is only one race, the human race. Only eight people got off the Ark and we are all descendants of them. We might look differently, act differently, or live in different environments, but that is because God made each individual unique. There will never be another Brewer, just as there will never be another BroJack. No two people will ever have the same fingerprints. I think we use racism as a cover to hide our feelings of hatred or anger brought on by some other situation in our lives, but we sometimes release those feelings under the disguise of racism. Amen?

Chapter 12

Salvation Is for Today

For He says, In the time of my favor I heard you, and in the day of salvation I helped you. I tell you, now is the time for God's favor, now is the day of salvation.

~ 2 Corinthians 6:2 ~

Steven Woods, Inmate # 999427

God offers salvation to all people. Many people put off a decision for Christ, thinking that there will be a better time, but they could easily miss their opportunity altogether. There is no guarantee that you will have the opportunity to convert before or even at the moment of death.

Steven Woods continued to put off the issue of his salvation because he was consumed with the unfairness of his situation. There comes a time in all of our lives when we will have to put aside the things of this world and address the question of eternity. In the end of our lives on Earth nothing about what happens here will really matter except our relationship with God.

CRIME CONVICTION: On May 2, 2001, in The Colony, Texas, Woods and one codefendant used a .380 caliber pistol, a .45 caliber pistol, and a knife to kill a twenty-one year old white male victim by shooting the victim six times in the head and cutting his neck four times. A nineteen-year-old white female victim was also killed, receiving two shots to the head, one shot in the knee, and having her throat cut. Woods and the codefendant took property from the victims, including their car keys, backpacks, a cell phone, and other personal items.

June 22, 2011

Today there was a new inmate on death watch named Steven Woods. I have already been warned by other inmates that he was a devil worshiper and that if I decided to talk to him I needed to be careful. I thought to myself, *Here we go again!*

As a servant of God, I do not get to choose to whom I tell the Gospel. Only God is worthy of making those decisions. So I headed to Steven's cell, expecting a rough initial meeting.

As I stopped at his cell door, he looked up from a letter he was writing and just stared at me. I try to look into an inmate's eyes when I first encounter them to see if I can see anything that would help me break the ice. I could tell immediately that this inmate did not want me there and that he was looking for a fight.

However, retreat is not an option for me so I said, "Hello. My name is Brother Jack. Most people call me BroJack for short and I am a volunteer chaplain. I am stopping by today to see if you would like to talk about anything."

He immediately replied, with a curt attitude, "We are talking right now, aren't we?"

I said, "I guess you are right. Would you like to talk about anything in particular?"

He said, "No!"

At this point, I was not going to give him the satisfaction of an argument so I said, "Well, I come here every week so I will keep stopping by in case you change your mind. Thank you for taking the time to talk to me." I looked him straight in the eye and smiled. I wanted him to know that I meant what I said. As I turned to move to the next cell, I could feel him staring at me and I realized that this inmate was going to be a challenge.

JUNE 29, 2011

Steven had just been brought back to his cell and as I approached him, I was trying to prepare myself for the worst; but then something miraculous happened. He was standing at his door waiting on me and to my surprise he said, "Hey, BroJack. How are you doing today?"

My heart started racing in my chest but I had to remain cool because it could be a setup. As I have mentioned before, when I walk up to an inmate's cell, the first thing I do is make sure I can see both of their hands. If I cannot, then I keep my distance from the cell until I can. Even though they are behind a steel door, they can still try to stab me with a homemade spear or throw bodily waste on me. The idea behind the bodily waste is to humiliate you and potentially cut your visit short.

I could see both of Steven's hands but I still approached with caution. I asked how he was doing and I could tell he was excited about something. Now here is an example of God's timing again! Steven had actually just returned from a visit with his attorneys and had received some very good news concerning his case. This had occurred at exactly the time that I was coming to his cell. I could tell he was bursting at the seams so I just listened as he started telling me his good news. As I was listening, I was also thanking God for allowing me to be here at this exact time. God had done it again!

He had received some good news concerning his case and it looked very likely that he would get a stay of execution. I told Steven what a wonderful blessing he had received today. He agreed and I knew I was taking a chance but I asked him where he believed that blessing came from.

He smiled and said, "I am not sure."

I smiled back and said, "Well, I am very happy for you. Do you mind if I come back to see you next week?"

He said, "Sure!"

I thanked him from the bottom of my heart for talking to me. Once again, God had opened a door and I intended to walk through it again next week. Glory Hallelujah!

JULY 27, 2011

Something is happening to Steven because he was waiting at his cell door for me to come by. He was smiling and immediately asked how I was doing. I told him I was about my Father's business as usual. We did not have long to talk because it was time for his shower and the guards were coming for him. I jokingly told him please do not miss his shower for the sake of everyone around.

He laughed and asked how *I* was doing. I said, "Great"!

Then I asked if we could talk about God and to my surprise, he said yes. I was going to ask him if he were to die today where would he go but bringing up death in this place is sometimes not cool. So I tried a different approach and asked him if he could remember a time in his life that he accepted God's gift of eternal life. Then he really surprised me and said yes! Just then, the guards came for his shower and I asked if I could pray for him. He agreed and after our prayer, I asked him if he did not

174

mind could we talk more about his salvation next week. He said he was not going anywhere and that he would be there. I laughed and moved to the next cell.

This just goes to show you that you have to be careful about listening to the opinions of other people. I do not know if Steven worships satan but I do know that he now faces a man of God and my God is bigger than the enemy. My visits with Steven should be very interesting over the next few weeks.

AUGUST 3, 2011

Today as I approached Steven's cell, he was waiting on me again! He is next in line for execution on September 13, just a little over a month from now. I feel like he is loosening up. I have been able to bring Jesus into our previous conversations but I am still not sure Steven is saved. After all, he is supposed to be a satan worshiper but after spending time with him, I don't feel like that is the case. Sometimes inmates create this false persona to keep other inmates from messing with them.

Steven seemed to be in a good mood today and he was more interested in what I had been doing. When I find myself in these types of conversations, I have to be careful not to reveal too much about my personal life. Even though these guys are in lockdown twenty-four hours a day, they still have ways of reaching the outside world. I directed the conversation back to him by asking about his family. I saw his eyes light up when he started talking about his daughter.

Sometimes I have to remind myself that I am face-to-face with a man who was convicted of cutting two people's throats and then shooting them several times. However, even these individuals have people in their lives that they actually love. I listened to Steven talk about his family and when he was finished, I asked if he would like to pray. He quickly said no and smiled.

That almost confirms my suspicions that he does not know Jesus as his Lord and Savior, however, there are days when I struggle with prayer myself so I have to be careful not to be too quick to judge. I told him I would be back next week and he thanked me for talking to him.

AUGUST 10, 2011

Today as I looked into Steven's cell, he was sound asleep, so I decided not to wake him. I know time is short but I have to be careful not to alienate him. I still have high hopes that I will get a chance to deliver the Gospel of Jesus Christ to this man. We will see!

AUGUST 24, 2011

It has been a few weeks since I have been able to talk to Steven so I am really praying that I will get an opportunity today. He has a little less than three weeks to live unless he receives a stay.

Hallelujah! He met me at his cell door, which was a good sign. I asked how he was doing and he starting talking about his family. I can always see his eyes light up when he talks about his family. I basically just let him talk. Most of those guys don't really want to hear about my life but want to either vent about their current situation or talk about themselves. I am glad to be there so they can cast their cares upon me.

I am still trying to get a chance to present the Gospel to Steven, to make sure he can know he is saved. He told me that he would listen as his execution draws closer. It is very close now if you ask me, but I need to wait on God's timing. I feel like it will be next week. I hope I am not too late. This time, though, Steven did let me pray for him and after I prayed, I was so thankful that almost I floated to the next cell!

AUGUST 31, 2011

I felt like today was going to be a good visit with Steven because when he heard me coming, he was waiting on me. I asked how he was doing and he said all right considering the circumstances. I somehow get the feeling that Steven is not afraid to die but I also do not know if he is saved. Remember, he was the devil worshiper everyone was talking about. I am more and more convinced that it is a front he was putting on to keep other inmates away from him.

I asked him if he had a chance to think about letting me present the Gospel to him and he said he would be ready next week. I did not rush him because I did not want to risk pushing him away. We have come a long way in a short time. In the beginning, he would not even allow me to mention God. Now he has agreed to let me present the Gospel to him next Wednesday. I pray to God that nothing goes wrong and I get the opportunity. I always have to remind myself that I cannot save anyone. I can only present the Gospel and tell someone how they can be saved. Only the Holy Spirit of God can save.

I was out of time so I prayed for Steven and told him good-bye. I thought I was done for the day but little did I know the guard who had been escorting me was having problems of her own and wanted to talk to me about them. She started telling me about her eleven-year-old daughter who had severe health problems. Twice the little girl had major surgeries and almost died both times.

Also, the guard's nine-year-son has severe asthma and uses a breathing apparatus to help him when he has attacks. I could see the pain in her eyes and I felt that she was exhausted. I asked if she would mind if I prayed for them and her. She smiled and said that she was hoping that I would. I stopped right there and prayed so I would not forget. I have learned that when someone needs prayer, it is best to do it right away because the chances of remembering later are slim and prayer is too important and powerful to be forgotten.

I felt good about my visit today, especially the fact that a guard reached out to me. God is good!

SEPTEMBER 7, 2011

Today is my last chance to present the Gospel of Jesus Christ to Steven and praise God he was waiting on me at his cell door. I was worried that he might not want to talk to me because he had just finished visiting with his mother and it could possibly have been their last visit. As I approached his cell, he smiled and said, "Good to see you, BroJack."

My heart was pounding but I did not want to jump right in so I asked how his visit with his mother went. He said he and his mother had a wonderful time. I was glad to hear that and I asked how he was feeling. He said he was nervous about next week so I used that as an opening to bring Jesus into the conversation.

I asked, "Can I talk to you about your salvation for just a minute?"

He smiled and said, "Sure, I am ready to listen."

I started by asking if he would like to be sure of where he goes when he leaves this Earth. He said yes so I proceeded to take him down the Romans Road. I ended with Romans 10:9. I told him only he could save himself and he could do so by agreeing with that one scripture (Romans 10:9), by praying to God and accepting Jesus into his life as Lord and Savior.

Steven listened to every word and seemed on the surface to really be thinking about what I had just told him. I will be praying for him and his salvation. I said my good-byes to Steven, possibly for the last time on this Earth. I could not resist making one last statement. I said, "Please think about what we have been talking about. Trust me; you do not want to leave this world without Jesus Christ."

He smiled and said, "Okay, BroJack. Hopefully I will see you next week."

I just smiled and shook his finger. For some reason, I felt like this would be the last time I would see him but only God knows from this point on. I cannot dwell on that part of this ministry.

*UPDATE: STEVEN WOODS

TEXAS EXECUTION IS FIRST OF 4 SCHEDULED OVER 2 WEEKS

By Antoinette Campbell, CNN

September 14, 2011 — Updated 0008 GMT (0808 HKT)

The Texas high court rejected a stay of execution for Steven Woods, now 31, who was convicted in two murders.

(CNN) — Texas is set to execute four inmates over two weeks, including one who died by injection Tuesday evening and another execution scheduled in the next two days.

Steven Michael Woods, Jr., was pronounced dead at 6:22 p.m., 10 minutes after the lethal injection dose began, said Michelle Lyons, a spokeswoman for the Texas Department of Criminal Justice. It was the 10th execution carried out in Texas this year.

"You're not about to witness an execution. You are about to witness a murder," Woods said before he was injected, according to Lyons. Woods added that his codefendant was the one responsible for two 2001 killings, she said. Earlier Tuesday, the state's high court rejected a stay of execution for Woods.

"We're disappointed in the outcome," attorney Brad Levenson said after the court's decision. His office had filed for a stay of execution on grounds of juror bias. Woods was sentenced to death for the slayings of 21-year-old Ronald Whitehead and 19-year-old Bethena Brosz in 2002. Codefendant Marcus Rhodes was sentenced to life in prison. Woods' execution Tuesday night was the 235th for Perry in his 11 years as the governor.

CNN's Nick Valencia contributed to this report.

http://edition.cnn.com/2011/CRIME/09/13/texas.executions

HIS OFFICIAL LAST STATEMENT:

You're not about to witness an execution, you are about to witness a murder. I am strapped down for something Marcus Rhodes did. I never killed anybody, ever. I love you, Mom. I love you, Tali. This is wrong. This whole thing is wrong. I can't believe you are going to let Marcus Rhodes walk around free. Justice has let me down. Somebody completely screwed this up. I love you too, Mom. Well, Warden, if you are going to murder someone, go ahead and do it. Pull the trigger. It's coming. I can feel it coming. Good-bye.

BROJACK'S FINAL COMMENTS:

Steven had told me on our last visit that he had interviewed with Ray Hill, who has a local radio show called "Execution Watch." I sometimes listen to it because on the day of a scheduled execution they broadcast live from 6:00 to 7:00 p.m. to provide coverage of executions. That is how I usually find out if an inmate is executed or receives a stay. Hill has someone stationed outside of Huntsville Prison to relay information back to him.

I listened last night as they announced that Steven had been executed. However, I think Ray Hill, who hosted this program, did something for the first time. He played the interview between him and

Steven in its entirety. I have to say it was a very good interview. It was around twenty minutes long and I thought Mr. Hill was very respectful and was there to allow Steven to speak his piece.

It was very hard to listen to this interview because you could tell Steven still had hope at the time of the interview, but today he is dead. One thing that he said will stay with me the rest of my life. He said, "Drugs put me here."

I will miss talking to Steven and I pray that he listened during our last visit concerning his salvation. Whether he is innocent or guilty does not matter now; only his salvation matters. I pray that I will see him on the streets of Glory someday.

If Steven murdered two people, then why? He falls into the category of a lot of others on the row: *Robbery to feed drug addiction!* When the enemy can gain control of your mind through drugs or alcohol, then you are fair game to do his bidding. Such was the case of Steven Woods.

Chapter 13

You've Got a Friend

Be devoted to one another in brotherly love. Honor one another above yourselves.

~ Romans 12:10 ~

Cleve (Sarge) Foster, Inmate # 999470

I have found a friend in one of the worst places on Earth, death row in the State of Texas. Cleve (Sarge) Foster was the first inmate I met when I entered death row for the first time two years ago. I saved Sarge's story for last because he and I had become close brothers in Christ over the last two years. We had plans to evangelize throughout the world when he got out. Yes, you heard me right, when he got out. Sarge had faith that his conviction would be overturned and he would be set free. He was very adamant about his innocence. Who am I to judge one way or another? If God sets him free then we will tell the world about the mercy of God. Only time will tell.

CRIME CONVICTION: In 2002, he and another man sexually assaulted and shot a twenty-eight-year-old black female, resulting in her death. They discarded the body in a ditch where it was discovered by workers who were laying pipe.

DECEMBER 7, 2010
FIRST EXECUTION EXPERIENCE

I met Cleve (Sarge) Foster for the first time today. He was already on A pod in the death-watch section awaiting execution. He is scheduled to be executed January 11, 2011, a little over a month from now. He is called Sarge because he spent twenty-one years in the US Army. At the time of his crime, he was an Army recruiter in the Fort Worth, Texas area.

He is a big man with a rugged face but you could still see fear and stress in his eyes. He was shirtless and dressed only in boxer shorts. As he approached his cell door, I backed up, not knowing what to expect. After only a few moments of talking to him, I relaxed a little, but only a little!

I introduced myself and after a little sizing-up by both of us, he started talking freely with me about the twenty-one years he spent in the Army.

Eventually I asked how he was doing and he simply replied, "I haven't been sleeping very well lately." I asked subtle questions about his relationship with God and he showed me some Christian literature that someone had brought to his cell. As our conversation came to an end, I gave him Romans 10:9 to read and he wrote it down and said he would. I asked if I could pray with him and he agreed. He stuck his fingertip through the wire-mesh window and I grabbed it for our prayer. As I held on, I could not help but think that the life in this small fingertip would most likely be gone in just over a month.

I pray that next Tuesday I get to go back and speak to Sarge more firmly about his salvation. My time on death row was up for the day and I was escorted back to One Building, the main entry point of the prison. As I walked through that last door to freedom, I realized how blessed I was to get in my car and drive home to my sons.

Freedom is something most of us take for granted. I never made a sound during the fifty-mile drive home. This first prison visit had made a dramatic impression on me and I had a lot on my mind. I did talk to God briefly to thank Him for allowing me to go into this place. Amen.

DECEMBER 14, 2010

Today I am very excited that I am going to get another chance to talk to Sarge. He has been in my thoughts and prayers all week and his salvation is all I can think about. I was so scared that he might be sleeping or he might not want to talk to me again but as the guard escorted me through the black steel door into his pod, he was anxiously waiting. Man, what a relief! I had one more chance to confront him about his salvation. As Sarge and I were talking, I waited for my chance to ease Jesus into the conversation.

It seemed like the conversation was going on forever and finally I could not take it anymore and I blurted out, "Sarge, can I ask you a question about Jesus?"

To my relief, he said, "Sure."

I asked him if some time in his life had he ever given his life to Jesus Christ, ensuring his salvation? He quickly and boldly said yes!

Then I asked him what being saved meant to him. The reason I ask a person to explain what being saved means to them is because there are too many people, especially churchgoers, sitting in church on Sunday

185

mornings who think they are saved and they are not. The most common answer is, "I was baptized when I was young." It is very dangerous to live under that false belief that being baptized means you are saved. So when I witness to someone about Jesus I always make sure they understand what it means to be saved.

Sarge gave me the answer I was praying for. He said because of the sacrifice of Jesus Christ for our sins, if we put our faith in Him, we too could now be forgiven and receive God's gift of salvation, which he assured me that he had done. If I could have I would have done a back flip right there! My heart was filled with joy for this death-row inmate.

However, he continued to share something with me that just blew my mind further. He told me that eight years ago, when he first entered death row, all hope was lost and he was in the process of trying to kill himself when God intervened. He had a sharpened piece of plastic and he was trying to cut his veins open in his arm when a person on the radio he was listening to started talking about how he had almost committed suicide and how God had somehow stopped him. Sarge stopped his attempted suicide long enough to listen to the man's story. By the time the story was over, he had abandoned his suicide attempt and not long after that, he committed his life to Jesus Christ. Man, it does not get any better than that! What a moving testimony!

As my visit ended, I left Sarge with Revelation chapters 21 and 22 to read. Those two chapters give us a brief glimpse of what heaven will be like when we get there. I hope it gives him peace like it did Humberto Leal, knowing that soon he will get to walk through those wonderful gates of heaven into the arms of Jesus.

DECEMBER 21, 2010

Things seemed a little different on death row today. I cannot really explain it but it seemed like more inmates were out of their cells for their one hour a day of recreation. It may be because I decided to go in an hour earlier so I would have more time and hopefully visit more inmates. Also when I was entering one of the pods, the guards had seven inmates lined up against the wall, stripped of all their clothing. I was reminded that they have no rights at all in this place, especially no right to privacy.

My prison escort today through G-pop to death row was an interesting man who was actually a major of the guards. When it came time to put on my protective vest, he gave me an option whether to wear it or not. I asked him why I should wear the vest and he said because the inmates have figured out that they can make spears that will fit through the wire mesh of the small windows on each side of their cell doors. A few months back an inmate was able to stab a guard in the neck with one of these spears. I thought about it and decided not to wear the vest. I refuse to walk in fear.

The major also shared some more helpful information. When the inmates are out of their cells for their hour of recreation, they are housed separately in regular cells with only steel bars; these cells are called "day rooms." If you mistakenly get close enough to an inmate in one of the day rooms, he can potentially grab you, which is what happened to a volunteer a few years ago. The inmate stuck his hand out to shake hands and the volunteer instinctively gave him his hand. The inmate proceeded to twist the volunteer's arm until it came loose from the socket. As I slowly put both of my hands in my pockets, I thought to myself, *This is a handy piece of information to have!* Even though I decided not to wear the vest, I now had a more heightened sense of awareness and caution.

Today I visited Sarge first because of his upcoming execution, which was scheduled for January 11, 2011. However, I need to tell you about one of the guards assigned to escort me. It was a female guard and as I introduced myself, I told her that for nine years I was an associate pastor in Diboll, Texas. She smiled and said she lives in a town near there.

At this point, I asked if we could move away from the cells a little so the inmates could not hear our conversation. I was uncomfortable with the possibility of an inmate hearing this personal information. I learned in my training from the Texas Department of Criminal Justice that it was not a good idea to share too much personal information with the inmates.

After we moved to a safer distance from the cells, I asked her if she had ever been to Faith Family Church and to my surprise, she had. It turns out we knew some of the same people and we were at that church at the same time.

Now, let me sum all this up. I never dreamed I would be ministering to inmates on death row and now one of the guards assigned to escort me had been in the same church at the same time as me! Only God can orchestrate things like that! I ended up ministering to her because I found out she had not been going to church and I could sense her need to go. Everyone needs the fellowship of fellow Christians!

Now back to Sarge. He seemed to be in good spirits despite the fact that his execution was twenty-one days away. My primary purpose today was to find out if he had any family planning to attend his execution. He had told me previously that his people were from Kentucky and I wondered if they were going to make the trip. To my relief, he told me his mother was coming. He explained that his dad had an accident on his tractor and was confined to a wheelchair and could not make the trip. He explained that his mother and another relative would arrive two days before his execution and that the state would allow them to visit with him up to four hours a day for those two days. No physical contact though. They would visit by phone through a double Plexiglas window.

I could not help but get the idea by some of his comments that Sarge thought his lawyers might find a last minute loophole that would possibly delay his execution. Only God Almighty would know about that at this point. If nothing changes, I hope to see Sarge at least one more time and maybe twice before his execution. I pray that God will give me words of comfort that can only come from Him for the Sarge!

DECEMBER 28, 2010

Today Sarge seemed glad to see me as he stuck a fingertip through the wire mesh on the side of his door. Remember, this is their way of shaking hands. In addition, this is their way of having a little human physical contact because, besides the physical contact they get from the guards, they do not have the opportunity to touch another human. To us who are free, this might not seem like such a big deal but imagine no human contact for years and years. Even when family and friends come to the prison to visit, they cannot touch them. This should be a wake-up call for us to hug our children, our family, and friends, as much as possible because you never know when that privilege or opportunity will be gone!

Sarge's execution date is two weeks from today. He proceeded to tell me about his day. They came and got him at 9:00 a.m. and took him to another part of the prison to sign his fourteen-day paperwork. A portion of that paperwork authorizes the state to release his belongings to his mother after his execution. He told me with a smile on his face that they had surprisingly taken his shackles and handcuffs off while he was signing those papers. His comment was, "They are not really worried about me. They know I am not dangerous."

He said another preacher from Louisiana came by today to visit. He seemed happy about that. He then told me he had more relatives than just his mom coming to visit him before his execution. His sister and brother were coming, along with various cousins and other in-laws. Moreover, most importantly, his son was coming! I was both happy and sad for him at the same time. I cannot imagine visiting my sons before being executed. Some things are too unbearable and that would be one of them.

Sarge did have one request during this visit. He wanted to know if, as a last request, they would let him see the movie *The Passion of the Christ*. I said I would contact the chaplain with Sarge's request. I wanted to ask why he wanted to see that movie but I did not want to pry. I prayed with Sarge, then said good-bye, and moved on to the next cell. I hope to see Sarge one more time on this Earth.

JANUARY 11, 2011

Today is the scheduled execution date for Sarge. By the time I got to death row he had already been moved to the execution section of the prison in Huntsville, Texas. This is about a forty-five mile drive west on Highway 190. The prison was on lockdown last week so I could not visit with Sarge. If he is executed today, I missed my last chance to say good-bye.

Texas has had the opportunity to perfect their execution process because they have executed more inmates than any other state. I could sense a difference in the atmosphere on the row this evening. Everyone knew that Sarge was scheduled to be executed sometime after 6:00 p.m. I tried to imagine what was going through his mind. Was it fear or peace that it was finally going to be over?

Also things were a little different this time concerning my protective vest. On the last two visits, I had the option whether to wear the vest or not. This time, the guards took me to their office and put the vest on me themselves to ensure I was protected as much as possible. Because Sarge was so popular on the row there was a heightened sense of awareness for safety. I made a mental note to be particularly cautious during my visit this time.

In addition, I had recently learned about a chaplain who was severely injured a few years ago, which made the added precautions even more acceptable to me. Apparently, this chaplain had become close friends with one of the death-row inmates and had made the mistake of trusting him too much. On their last visit the day before his execution, the inmate asked the chaplain to pray for him but this time he wondered if they could hold hands as is customary among Christians in most places, but not on death row.

There used to be an opening under the inmate's cell door just wide enough for a hand to fit. The chaplain, not thinking clearly, got down on his hands and knees and stuck his arm through the opening so he could hold the hand of the inmate during their prayer. Immediately the inmate pulled his arm into his cell as far as he could and tied it to the toilet, which is close to the cell door. The inmate then proceeded to try to sever the chaplain's arm up to the elbow. I do not know what sort of device the inmate used, but it was effective enough to cut the chaplain's arm down to the bone. The chaplain survived the attack but died of a heart attack six months later. This was a hard lesson to learn, as I slowly double-checked my vest!

I put my mind back on the question: Will Sarge be executed today? I have no idea.

*UPDATE: CLEVE (SARGE) FOSTER:

The U.S. Supreme Court gave a last-minute stay of execution Tuesday evening to a Desert Storm veteran and former Army recruiter convicted of raping and killing a Sudanese immigrant in Fort Worth in 2002.

Cleve Foster, 47, known as "Sarge" on death row, had eaten his final meal and was waiting to walk a few steps to the death chamber when the court's brief order was received just before 6:00 p.m., a prison spokesman said.

The court offered no explanation for its decision or why justices other than Justice Antonin Scalia participated. Scalia can act alone on

Texas execution appeals. But he can also ask other justices to vote on whether to hear an appeal.

http://open.salon.com/blog/scottcobb/2011/01/12/photos_of_protest_at_te xas_capitol_of_scheduled_execution_of_cleve_foster_who_received_last _minute_stay

Wow! Sarge got a stay of execution at the last minute and his life was spared! I found this out almost immediately because I was monitoring the internet all evening on the day of his execution. I cannot wait until I get a chance to see him again. I have a thousand questions!

FEBRUARY 2, 2011
SECOND EXECUTION EXPERIENCE

I have not seen Sarge since his near execution so I had a million questions but was not sure if I should ask them. Since he does not have a new execution date, he is on B pod instead of deathwatch on A pod, so I made a special trip over there to see him.

When he first saw me today, he gave me this great big smile and shouted, "BroJack!"

I smiled back and said, "Hey, Sarge! Where you been?"

He laughed and said, "I been going to & fro brother! To & fro". I recognized this as a reference to what satan said to God when asked where he had been. Satan explained he had been going "to & fro" or back and forth between the earth and heaven. I thought this was a great analogy by Sarge considering he almost left earth to go to heaven!

He continued to explain that after he got his stay of execution on January 11, they took him to Fort Worth, Texas for some hearings concerning his appeal. However, it was not long before the Supreme Court rejected his appeal and sent him back to the row here in Livingston. He now has a new execution date of April 5, 2011!

As I looked at him, he knew I was busting at the seams to ask him some questions. So being the fearless person I am, I asked if he wanted to share with me about his near execution experience and he said he sure! He proceeded to explained it in great detail.

On the morning of his execution, they got him up early and after he showered and ate breakfast, they shackled him for the forty-five-mile ride to Huntsville prison. He said when he arrived at Huntsville, he was met by several guards, the warden, and two chaplains. The chaplains spent almost all of the day with him explaining what was going to happen. They told him that if he had not heard anything from his lawyer by 5:40 p.m., more than likely the execution would proceed. They went on to explain that when he heard footsteps behind the holding cell he was in, it would be the guards coming to get him for his execution. He laughed as he told me that every time he heard a noise behind the cell it got his full attention!

He was allowed to have a phone for most of the day to call anyone he wanted. He called and talked to his dad who could not make the trip because of his farm injury. I cannot imagine that conversation. What do you say to your dad when you are about to be executed and what does a dad say to his son in that situation. He said he called old girlfriends, old buddies, and anybody else he could think of. I thanked him for not calling me and he said something that almost made me cry. He said, "I do not need to say goodbye to you because I will see you again in the Kingdom of God".

A lot of his family had made the long trip from Kentucky to come to the execution. His mom, his son, and his son's fiancée, his two sisters, and other relatives were there. When he told me his son was there, I again could not imagine the conversations between them considering the circumstances. I did not know it but Sarge was about to *blow my mind!*

I asked him if he was scared at any time throughout this experience. He said no because he had made his peace with God and if it was his time to meet God face-to-face, then so be it. He said that 5:40 p.m. came and went and at about three minutes after 6:00 p.m., the warden stepped into his cell and handed him a phone. His lawyer was on the other end, and in a very emotional state, told him that the United States Supreme Court had granted him a stay of execution to review his appeal.

I asked him how he felt at that very moment and he said something that sent chills up my spine!

He said, "Now, BroJack, you can believe this next part or not, it doesn't matter to me, but I didn't feel anything emotionally, however physically, I could feel two hands, one under each arm, holding me up! It was then that I knew Jesus was right there with me holding me up through this very difficult time in my life. I could literally feel His hands pressing into my sides and holding me up!"

When he told me that, I had chills all over my body and a golf-ball-size lump in my throat, and all I could think of was what a loving God we serve. I believed Sarge with all my heart because what he said makes sense. The Bible says that to be absent from the body is to be present with the Lord (2 Corinthians 5:8).

I also believe Jesus is there to make the transition from this world to heaven easy. He does not want us to be afraid. I remembered that each time God sent the Angel Gabriel to talk with someone his first words were usually, Do not be afraid.

I would like to have stayed longer for my visit with Sarge but it was time to move on. I thanked Sarge for being so honest with me and I told him I would be back. I now had a different view of death after what Sarge told me. It did not seem quit as scary as before.

FEBRUARY 8, 2011

I did not know it in advance but today God was about to use an inmate on death row in Texas to witness to me. As you know, Sarge was scheduled to be executed on January 11, 2011, but got a stay of execution at the last moment. However, the United States Supreme court denied the stay and he was sent back to death row in Livingston. His new execution date was rescheduled for April 5, 2011.

Here is a prime example of God's timing. As I was talking to another inmate, I heard the guards bringing an inmate onto deathwatch. I looked out of the corner of my eye because I did not want to take my eyes off the inmate I was talking to at the time, and low and behold, it was 'The Sarge'! They brought him to the landing at the top of the second tier, which was about ten feet from me. This was the first time I had seen Sarge out of his cell and he did not look as big standing there in shackles surrounded by guards. They did not have his cell ready so he had to stand there waiting for a good twenty minutes, which allowed me time to finish my visits with some other inmates.

As I finally made it to Sarge's cell, he was smiling from ear to ear. I asked him what was going on. He began to explain how he was so afraid that he was not going to get a chance to see me again. He said he could not believe it when he started walking up those stairs and there I was, at the exact day and time he was being moved from B pod back to A pod deathwatch. I had to admit to myself that it seemed God had orchestrated this encounter. For Sarge to be moved to his new cell on the exact date and time I was on the deathwatch section of death row was pretty amazing.

Sarge began to tell me that God had spoken to him about me and that he needed desperately to tell me something. At this point, I know what some of you must be thinking: Sarge is trying to gain my confidence in order to get something from me later. I did not believe that at this point however I am not about to let my guard down either. And besides, I don't have anything to offer him except the knowledge of how to make Jesus Christ Lord and Savior over his life.

Sarge started to explain that after he talked to me last week about his encounter with God on his scheduled execution date he felt like God told him he was not finished and that he had not told me everything. If you remember, he told me how when he received the news that he had received a stay of execution all he could feel were two hands holding him up. He went on to explain that it was more like his whole body was being held in the palms of two loving hands and that God wanted me to know that those same two loving hands were holding me up in whatever I was going through.

I could sense a passion in Sarge that I had not seen before in him but I have seen this passion elsewhere. It is the passion that comes from knowing God is using you to minister to someone. To me there is nothing more satisfying than knowing that God, the Creator of the universe, would use someone like me to minister to one of His children. I could tell Sarge felt that way, too. He was very excited that God would use a condemned man to minister to someone else. It just goes to show you that God can use you right up to the last breath for His glory.

It turns out that I am struggling with some things right now but Sarge does not know that. I never tell any inmate my personal business for obvious reasons. So today, God used a condemned man on death row to speak to my heart concerning my current struggles. By the way, we are all condemned and under a death sentence. It is only by the shed blood of Jesus that we are saved! Just thought I would throw that in there for some reason.

I said thank you to Sarge and he seemed very happy that he had completed his assignment for God. He also told me that, based on the encounters he had been having with God, especially on the day of his "almost" execution; he is actually looking forward to going home to be with God. He said, "Look around me, BroJack. This is no way to live. If they are going to kill me, then I am ready. I have no fear and I thank God for showing me that there is no reason to be afraid. What a mighty God we serve!"

I found myself saying for the third time today on the row, "I love you, brother."

Sarge said, "I love you too, man" and I walked away wanting to find somewhere to cry. Sometimes God's mercy and love are overwhelming.

MARCH 1, 2011

I have been locked out of the prison for two weeks and I was excited about being back on the row. Today as I entered the prison, things seemed different but that was not unusual. Things are different in some way every time I go into the prison. I had no problem getting a "ride" to the row but after I checked into the guard station, I experienced something that had not happened before. I checked into the guard station to get an escort and was told to just go to a pod and they would give me an escort on the pod. That meant I was basically free to roam the hallways alone. I felt a little nervous until I remembered that it was God who sent me there. If God is for me then who can be against me! However, I did take the time to remind God that it was just Him and me today and that my life was totally in His hands.

As I entered deathwatch on A pod, someone from one of the cells shouted, "Hey, BroJack!" I could not tell who it was, so I shouted, "What's up?" and proceeded to that cell first. To my excitement, it was Sarge. He was in a different cell from last week. He immediately showed me two paintings he was working on and I have to tell you they were very good. I do not know if they were the kind you paint by the numbers but, either way, I was impressed. Because Sarge was a model inmate, he was allowed the extra privilege of painting pictures in his cell.

We talked a little longer and then suddenly I heard a lot of noise coming from out in the hallway. A guard came up to my escort and informed him that he was needed in another area and asked me to return to the control booth. And just like that I had to cut my visit short with Sarge, which was a little disappointing.

MARCH 8, 2011

Today, as I went through the steel door onto A pod, I saw Sarge waiting on me from his cell. He seemed happy to see me. He started telling me about how he had been witnessing to other inmates about his experience with God on January 11, when he was supposed to be executed. He was sharing with other inmates about how he could literally feel God's hands around him as the time for his execution drew near.

He also told me that some people from Bill Glass Ministries came on the row and sang some songs for the inmates. I thought that was wonderful! Sarge said even some of the hardcore inmates had tears in their eyes. Praise God for that ministry!

Sarge then shared something about his son that touched my heart. After Sarge got a stay of execution on January 11, he talked to his son later that day and his son said, "Dad, I think it is time for me to put God back in my life." I could see the excitement and pride in Sarge's face as he was telling me about his son. A father's pride! There is nothing like it.

I asked to see the pictures he was painting when I visited him last week and as he showed them to me, my heart sank thinking about what could have been, concerning the life of Cleve (Sarge) Foster. They were very good paintings.

Sarge has a new execution date of April 5, 2011. I cannot imagine going through the execution process once, much less twice. As I said good-bye, I told him I would do my best to see him as many times as possible before April 5. Only God knows what will happen on that day. Once again, it was time for me to leave death row. On the way home, I cried. I do not know why. I just did.

MARCH 15, 2011

Today, as usual, Sarge was smiling ear to ear when he saw me. He said, "What's up, BroJack?" I said, "Aw, you know, the same old thing. It's all good."

He started telling me about a dream he had a few nights before. He and his son were getting into his pickup truck back in the Kentucky hills. In the distance, he saw a pack of black wolves staring at him. He felt like the lead one was satan himself and they were waiting for his son and him to turn their backs. Sarge knew that, if they did, they would be attacked. He and his son got into the truck and drove like the wind to get away. Sarge said for a brief moment he knew what it felt like to be free again. We both agreed that one day when we get to heaven; we will know what it is like to be truly free!

He seemed a little down after he shared that dream with me and he started talking about how he periodically gets depressed when the reality of the row and his situation sets in. He tries to keep his mind occupied but it is not easy when hour after hour there is nothing. I cannot imagine the loneliness. He again stated that he should not even be there and that is the most frustrating thing of all. He told me that the row is an evil place and said, "You can believe me or not but at night I constantly watch dark shadows pass by from underneath my door." He knew they were not guards because you can hear them coming in this all-metal environment. I told him I believed him. This is prime satan real estate.

He then lightened the mood a little by sharing what he plans to do at his execution. Last time he got a stay at the last moment but he said before it was time to execute him they stripped him down to search him. He found himself standing naked before twenty or so people who are involved in the execution process. He said this time he plans to mark his butt with a marker with the words "Kiss" on the left cheek and "Me" on the right cheek! I laughed for five minutes. I wish I could be there to see their faces!

Then he told me a joke! "How much cocaine can Charlie Sheen do? Enough to kill *Two and a Half Men*!" Again I laughed.

Once again, it was time to leave the row and the Polunsky Unit State Prison. As I walked past the last checkpoint and arrived outside, I felt especially grateful that I was a free man. Thank you God for something we take for granted only too often — our *freedom*!

MARCH 22, 2011

Today Sarge was happy to see me because he said he wanted to talk to me about something important. He asked me what I was doing next Tuesday; which caught me off guard. I said I would probably be here on the row. He said he wanted me to meet his family when they came from Kentucky for his execution. I almost broke down and cried but I managed to maintain my composure somehow. The fact that he thought enough of me to want me to meet his family was very humbling. It broke my heart to tell him that I could not. The Texas Department of Criminal Justice is very strict about a volunteer having any contact with any family member of an inmate.

Sarge seemed disappointed but then he said something else that really caught me off guard. Sarge had painted a picture that I really like and he said he wanted me to have it. Again, I had to tell him that I could not accept it because the TDCJ will not allow us to accept or give anything to an inmate. He then came up with a brilliant idea. He said he would give it to my church and then I could get it. I told him I would call the head prison Chaplain in the morning to see if that was acceptable. If so, I would give the Chaplain the address of my church so he could give it to Sarge. I was looking for a place to cry but I had to maintain my composure once again. I prayed with Sarge and told him I would see him next week if it were God's will.

I decided to leave the row a little early today because my heart was on overload and I needed some quiet time. As I drove home that night, I could not help but cry. This is reality and sometimes the reality of sin and this cruel world is overwhelming.

MARCH 29, 2011

Today Sarge was in a good mood. He had just come back from spending four hours on a special visit with his twenty-one year old son, who rode a Greyhound bus from Kentucky to see him. He talked about his son with a father's pride. I cannot imagine my sons and me spending time together knowing that I was scheduled to be executed in one week. What a horrible situation that would be.

Sarge then showed me the picture he wanted me to have. It was wrapped in a brown envelope and he wanted me verify the address of the church. It was correct and again I told him he should leave that picture to someone in his family but he insisted he wanted me to have it.

I listened to him talk for a while about things that he wanted to get off his chest and then he told me about his plan to help the Japanese and their recent nuclear reactor problem brought on by a powerful earthquake, followed by a devastating tsunami.

His plan was that he and Mark Stroman (we have read about Mark in Chapter 10), would volunteer to go to Japan and walk into those nuclear plants where no man can currently go for fear of deadly radiation exposure. They would fix the problems, thus sacrificing themselves and saving thousands of lives. It would be an honorable way to die instead of being executed by Texas. He joked about it but underneath I think he was serious.

I knew my time with Sarge was ending so I asked if I could pray with him. He quickly agreed and I prayed for my friend possibly for the last time. I held onto his fingertip that he had poked through the wire mesh on the side of his cell door just a little harder and longer this time. As I finished our prayer, I looked him straight in the eyes and said, "I love you brother."

He said, "I love you too, Brojack." I hope I see my friend again but only God knows for sure. If not, I will miss him.

Once again, I left the row today feeling sad. I cannot help it. I am a born-again, blood-bought, child of God, and I strive to see people the way God's sees them and I believe He is sad to see one of His children facing the wrath and judgment of man.

Side Note: I got a call today from Bro Vic Bass at Faith Family Church in Diboll, Texas. He said he got a letter from Sarge to the church. I told Sarge about the church but I had no idea he was going to write a letter to them. Bro Vic said he cried as he read it, his wife cried, and the church secretary cried. I told him not give it to me until after next week. Sarge may or may not be alive after next Tuesday so I do not want any more sad thoughts running through my mind. I will wait until after next Tuesday to read his letter.

APRIL 5, 2011

Today Sarge is scheduled to be executed. This is his second trip to the execution chamber. I struggled about going to the row today because usually either the prison is on lock down or the inmates are in a bad mood because it is an execution day.

My routine on the days I visit death row, as I have mentioned before, is that I drive from Houston to Livingston. That is about a fifty-mile trip one-way. On the drive up there, I decided to call a friend in Florida to see if they heard anything on the internet or the national news about a stay of execution for Sarge. Sometimes people in other states have access to information before people in Texas.

I almost fainted when my friend told me that a newspaper in Texas and some articles on the internet were reporting that Sarge got a stay already. Usually a stay of execution comes in the final hours from 4:00 p.m. to 6:00 p.m. Last time on January 11, 2011, his stay came at 6:03 p.m., as he was getting ready to enter the death chamber. I asked my friend if they were sure and they replied, "Yes!"

I felt relieved but deep down inside I was not going to believe it until I got to the prison and saw for myself.

As I arrived on death row, I asked the first guard I saw about Sarge and he said he received a stay. I was very happy for him but I quickly reminded myself that there was an innocent dead woman in all of this. I never want to forget the victims.

*UPDATE: CLEVE (SARGE) FOSTER:

For the second time, the U.S. Supreme Court gave a last-minute stay of execution Tuesday evening to a Desert Storm veteran and former Army recruiter convicted of raping and killing a Sudanese immigrant in Fort Worth in 2002.

I was surprised when the guard told me Sarge was on B pod. I did not understand how he got back to the prison so fast. As I was escorted up the steel stairs to the second tier of B pod, I saw Sarge smiling through the eight-inch slot on the side of his cell door. I just looked into his big smiling face and asked what happened. He said he did not even leave death row. The warden gave him a phone call from his lawyer around 10:30 a.m. who told him the United States Supreme Court had once again given him a stay and this time it was better than before. This time it was based on whether he received adequate counsel during the course of the case, as well as questions related to his guilt. Who knows what will happen now. It could mean a new trial, which could mean acquittal, or the stay could be rejected and Sarge would receive a new execution date. What a roller coaster ride! I think about the agony that Sarge's family is suffering but I also think about the family of the victim who deserve justice for their loved one. So many people suffer because of sin. It is hard to comprehend sometimes.

I talked to Sarge for a while and then the guard told me an inmate down the tier wanted to talk to me. I said my good-byes to Sarge and followed the guard. Man, what a ride!

Side Note: Now that Cleve is still alive, I can read his letter to Faith Family Church:

> *24 Mar 11, day 3289, 21:31*
>
> *Dear Pastor Vick,*
>
> *Hi! You don't know me but most call me "Sarge" and that's because of my 21 years in the Army "Hooah!" I'm writing you for a few reasons. 1st to thank you and your church for having such great people.*
>
> *For about the past 5 months I've been blessed by God and he's done that by blessing your church and its people, and in return God's hand "through your church" have sent us "here on Death Row" a blessing "Brother Jack".... Ya see Pastor Vick, we on Death Row are not allowed to have church, so for the past 9 years all we get is an occasional passerby volunteer who for the most part never even remember our name, much less what we say. Never the less last October I was moved to death watch because I was given an execution date of Jan 11 and that's around the time I met Brother Jack and another volunteer*

"can't remember his name but both are so blessed and a blessing.

Pastor Vick, my church service comes to me on Tuesdays and for the most part less than 15 minutes and that service was Brother Jack. God's light shines through this man and there have been some days I really needed it.

I won't sit here and go on about Brother Jack because we all know that it's God who gets all the praise and I'm sure you agree, but it's the body of your church from which my dear brother in Christ comes and for that I thank you.

Another reason I am writing is because a few weeks ago I made a painting of a "Church in a Valley" and BroJack really liked it so seeing as how he can't accept things from us I'd like to donate this painting to your church.

I want my brother to know that every time he sees it I want it to remind him of home and should others ever stop and look at it I hope they think of home also. God's house is everyone's home.

I'm not sure just how long it will take to get to you because it has to go through the TDCJ process but I'm hoping not long. I do have a request. I'd like for you and your church to pray for me because I've another execution date of 5 April. I also ask that you pray for my family.

God gave me a miracle back in January and I'm sure praying for another one ... Ha-ha... Amen!

My family is coming all the way from Henderson, Kentucky and should be here on the 31st. So I'll tell them of your church and should they decide to visit your church my mom's name is Mary Ann Megan and she's my hero.

Now in closing I'm gonna give you a short word of testament. As I've told I did have an execution date of Jan 11 but God gave me a miracle. My execution should have happened at 18:00 (6 p.m.) but at 18:03 the call came in and my execution had been stayed. Let me tell you about it.

My entire life I've always known of God and as a young kid I gave my life to him. However! If backsliding were an Olympic sport I'd have a gold medal. But God's Word is true. He never left me nor has He ever forsaken me. And although I've many stories of His miracles in my life, the one on Jan 11, 2011 actually involved God's touch.

I arrived at the Wall's about 13:30 (Huntsville) and from the moment I arrived time clicked by so very fast. The officers were very professional and courteous and we all knew why I was there. "To be executed."

I walked in...smile on my face...and had the peace of God's Word promised. 1:30 p.m. to 5:30 p.m. went by in a flash. I'd made all my phone calls, had spoken to my spiritual advisor, and had picked at my last meal and had looked at the death chamber door several times. I was told that if the call had come in that my appeals were over, then at 5:40 p.m. I would walk into the most active death chamber America has ever known.

Well 5:40 p.m. came and nothing happened. I was told that when the time comes I'd hear footsteps coming from behind my cell. So every footstep I heard, time would stop. The Chaplains would tell me "No" this is not it and eventually I was told they had until midnight. Well, we continued to pray and wait. Then at 6:03 p.m. the phone rang. Time Stopped! It was like the matrix. Every move was like second by second.

The Chaplain picked up the phone and looked at me blank faced and held out the phone to me. I didn't want to take it at first but when I did I heard an emotional Attorney tell me, "Cleve, I don't know what happened but the Supreme Court gave you a stay."

Vick, I felt like a baby in my Father's hands. I thought I was going to cry but all I felt was love. My God, "The Father," had His hands wrapped around my entire body. It was like he was holding me up.

God's Word is true and NOBODY, not a single person can tell me otherwise.

Vick, I've told my story to Brojack and when I did you could see the spark in his eyes and at that moment I felt led by God to tell Brojack that. God has His hands on him as well but something came up and Brojack had to leave. But the next Tuesday he came in and the first thing he said was tell me again. I did and before he could speak I told him, "Hold on, Brojack, last week you had to leave before I could tell you. God wanted me to tell you that His hands are around you as always and He loves us all.

Pastor Vick, I've told this to countless inmates already and when they moved me back to death watch I told them also.

Just two days ago a guy came to death watch and he stood out in the day room and said, "Gosh! This is not like I expected death watch to be. Doom and gloom. NOT! When I went to the day room next I let him know why. God is here! We laughed, we openly talked of God and His glory and mercy.

Vick, you can hear a pin drop every time I tell people of my Jan 11 execution date. Pastor Vick, I'm 6ft 270 lbs, with a military voice. I tell people like it is. I love God and he loves us all.

I won't take up any more of your time but I will thank you in advance for the prayers. I'm on Twitter and Facebook. Pastor Vick, thanks again for everything and enjoy the painting.

God bless you and yours
Sargent

THIRD EXECUTION EXPERIENCE

Once again, Sarge's appeals were denied and he has a new execution date of September 20, 2011. Over the next several months, I would continue my weekly visits with Sarge and we would become closer and closer. We made plans to go on this evangelism tour together if he ever got out of prison.

Who knows at this point? He has already received two stays of execution. Maybe he will get a new trial and be set free. It has happened before!

We have these big dreams of touring the world and witnessing to the lost using our experiences. What a powerful testimony to Jesus that would be. We have it planned where we will have this mock prison cell on stage and we will share the Gospel of Jesus Christ through the cell door just as we do now. I hope that it will happen but I have learned not to get my hopes built up when it comes to what will happen inside these prison walls. There is absolutely no way of knowing if Sarge will be executed this third time.

SEPTEMBER 14, 2011

For months now, Sarge and I have had some great times during our visits but now it was time to face his third execution date. Today as I approached his cell, Sarge was waiting at his door and he immediately stuck his fingertip through the wire mesh and I immediately shook it. I had decided to try not to talk about his scheduled execution next Tuesday but rather try to give him some sort of hope. So, I started talking about our evangelism tour when he gets out of prison. We tossed ideas back and forth for almost an hour. And for that hour he had hope.

Finally, though, I had to say something in case this was the last time I saw him on this Earth. As I was fighting back the tears, I said, "Sarge ... I don't know what is going to happen next week but I want you to know this. I will never forget you and your story will be told everywhere God sends me to preach His Word. I want to thank you for being so nice to me. You are the first inmate I met when I came in here almost a year ago. You have become as good a friend as I have ever had. I look forward to coming to see you each week and you have been a blessing to me. Please do not forget me and I know with confidence that we will meet again on the streets of Glory someday. We will not remember this mess but we will remember that we were not just friends, but *good* friends. I love you and God bless you my brother!"

He had tears in his eyes as he said, "You have been a good friend to me too, BroJack. No one else would spend the time you have with me, especially in a place like this. You put yourself in danger every week and you keep coming back. I pray for God's blessing on you. Can you do one last thing for me?"

I said, "What is it?"

He replied with a message for Buck, another inmate who is scheduled to be executed tomorrow. "Tell Buck that if he enters the death chamber, tell him to plead the blood of Jesus over the entry door so that no one else will walk through that door without knowing Jesus. And if he doesn't get the chance, I'll do it myself next week, if it is the will of God." Wow! How powerful is that! To have the presence of mind to think of the salvation of others when you are facing the end of your own mortality. I only hope that when my time comes I am half the Christian Sarge is.

I asked if we could pray and he said, "Please do."

I prayed a long and slow prayer this time, hoping to remember everything that needed to be asked of God concerning Sarge's future. Finally, it was time to leave my friend for perhaps the last time. I had been talking to Sarge for over ninety minutes but it seemed like only five. I mustered up the strength to turn and walk away. What a miserable situation. I do not know what to do about the pain and sorrow I feel in the pit of my stomach.

*UPDATE: CLEVE FOSTER

COURT HALTS EXECUTION OF TEXAS INMATE
CLEVE FOSTER

By Edecio Martinez Sept. 20, 2011

(CBS/AP) Livingston, Texas — Cleve Foster, a former Army recruiter who for the third time this year was hours away from his scheduled execution for the rape-slaying of a woman in Fort Worth nearly 10 years ago, was granted yet another reprieve by the U.S. Supreme Court on Tuesday.

The 47-year-old was set to die Tuesday evening in Huntsville.

The high court twice earlier this year stopped Foster's scheduled lethal injection. The latest court ruling came about 2 1/2 hours before Foster could have been taken to the Texas death chamber.

Foster was meeting with one of his lawyers in a small holding cell a few feet from the death chamber when a Texas Department of Criminal Justice spokesman delivered the news.

"He thanked God and pointed to his attorney, saying this woman helped save his life," prison spokesman Jason Clark said.

He also said Foster repeated his insistence that he was innocent.

Unlike his previous trips to the death house in Huntsville, the reprieve came before he was served his requested final meal, which included two fried chickens and a five-gallon bucket of peaches.

Instead, he immediately was returned to death row at a prison about 45 miles to the east.

Foster was one of two men convicted and sent to death row for fatally shooting a 30-year-old woman whose body was found in a ditch by pipeline workers in Fort Worth in February 2002. His partner died last year of cancer.

http://www.cbsnews.com/8301-504083_162-20109345-504083.html

Conclusion

A Time to Stop

He upholds the cause of the oppressed and gives food to the hungry. The
Lord sets prisoners free.
~ Psalm 146:7 ~

I would like to take credit for some of the miraculous things that have taken place since I have been going into death row but the truth of the matter is the Lord Jesus Christ deserves all the glory.

After Cleve (Sarge) Foster went to the death chamber at the Huntsville Prison for a third time on September 20, 2011, and received a stay of execution for the third time, I decided that I would make that event a stopping point for this book. I could go on writing about the men on death row in Texas indefinitely because I do not see an end to the death penalty any time soon in Texas and I do not see an end to people stopping the violent act of murder.

Even though I have stopped writing about it, I am still going into death row and have been for over two years now. Every time I feel that I cannot take any more of this ministry because of all the sadness and anxiety associated with it, God gives me the strength to go back one more time.

Over the last two years, I have had conversations or encounters with over two hundred of the over three hundred inmates currently housed on death row in Texas. Thirty-one of them have been executed. I am constantly getting questions about how I feel about that. I do not think any single statement can explain the full gambit of emotions associated with the execution of a fellow human being. One week you are having a conversation with someone and the next week they're gone forever. There is no way to digest or even process something like that.

I have met men of God in this place and I have met men of satan. After a while, it becomes obvious which men belong to God and which ones serve the enemy. I have learned more about witnessing and presenting the Gospel of Jesus Christ on death row than I ever would had I stayed an associate pastor of a church. You are on the front lines, on death row, and you have to be ready for almost anything. I never know what to expect any time I visit death row.

Do I have more compassion now than before I entered death row? Without a doubt, I am a different person. I have a deeper compassion for these inmates but I also have a deeper compassion for their victims and for the families on both sides. Murder is a horrible thing and it destroys the lives of the innocent as well as the guilty. It is a nightmare for all involved.

Have my visits to death row over these last two years changed my opinion concerning the death penalty? I do not think so. I am still as confused about it as ever. I know the anger that murder creates for the families of the victims because I myself am a victim of violent crimes. Nevertheless, is execution right or wrong? The Word of God says:

Whoever sheds man's blood,

By man his blood shall be shed;

For in the image of God He made man (Genesis 9:6)

In the first two lines of this verse God says if you take another person's life man will take yours, seemingly justifying the death penalty.

Jesus also said, *"For all who take the sword will perish by the sword"* (Matthew 26:52). This would seem to justify executing a person for murder as well.

However, on the other hand, God also says, *"The Lord is not slow in keeping his promise, as some understand slowness. Instead he is patient with you, not wanting anyone to perish, but everyone to come to repentance"* (2 Peter 3:9). This verse indicates that God does not want anyone to perish, but for everyone to be saved. Besides being one of the Ten Commandments (*thou shall not kill*), He goes on to say in the last line of Genesis 9:6, *"for in the image of God He made man,"* indicating to kill a person is to kill one made in God's image. When we interact with others, we are interacting with beings made by God, beings to whom God offers eternal life, beings that God has plans to use to witness to a lost world.

I interpret all of this to mean that God does not condone murder and you will suffer at the hands of man for such an act, but because of God's grace, even murderers can receive God's gift of salvation through the shed blood of His Son Jesus Christ.

Does that seem fair? It depends on from whose eyes you are viewing it. The families left behind as a result of this violent act may think this gift of salvation is unfair but those who have totally committed to God will leave those types of judgments to God Almighty Himself.

Do I think executing a human being is cruel and unusual punishment? After entering death row on a weekly basis for over two years, I do not think the execution itself is cruel, but the way the inmates live for an average of ten years on death row before they are finally executed is cruel. So, if it is any consolation to the families of the victims of the violent crimes these men committed, they live in a daily nightmare and I would rather leave this world by execution than spend one minute locked up on death row in the State of Texas!

In hopes of perhaps easing the pain of my mother's murder, am I any closer to understanding why a person murders another? I have learned several reasons why people murder and I have gotten to know many murderers. Not just in passing, but I have spent hour after hour talking with them and my conclusion is this: They do not seem much different from the people I meet and talk to in the outside world every day. I still believe, given the right circumstances, we are all capable of murder whether we want to believe it or not. It comes from the sinful nature we are all born with. Only God can change it! But only you can make that choice to let Him.

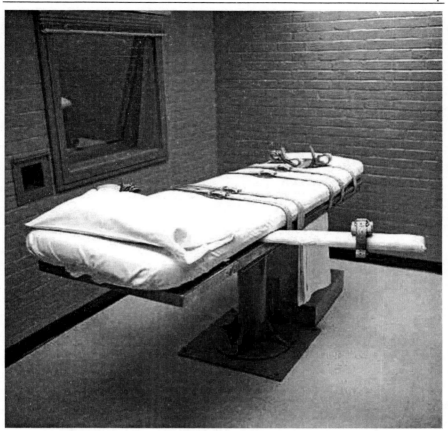

THE FINAL STOP

*FINAL UPDATE: CLEVE (SARGE) FOSTER

TEXAS PUTS TO DEATH MAN WHO RECEIVED THREE STAYS OF EXECUTION

Tue Sep 25, 2012 9:19 p.m. EDT

(Reuters) — Texas executed a man on Tuesday who had received three stays of execution from the U.S. Supreme Court because of questions about how forcefully his lawyers defended him.

Cleve Foster, 48, was convicted with an accomplice in the 2002 murder and rape of Nyanuer "Mary" Pal, whose naked body was found in a ditch, according to a report by the Texas Attorney General's office.

Foster had asked the U.S. high court for a fourth stay of execution but it was denied on Tuesday. He was pronounced dead at 6:43 p.m. local time (2343 GMT) at the state penitentiary in Huntsville, Texas, criminal justice spokesman Jason Clark said.

The U.S. Supreme Court a year ago, granted a temporary stay of execution just 2 1/2 hours before Foster was to be put to death by injection. It was the third stay from the high court for Foster, who also was granted delays in January and April 2011.

Tuesday's request for a fourth stay was referred by Justice Antonin Scalia to the full court but just three of the nine justices, Elena Kagan, Sonia Sotomayor, and Ruth Bader Ginsburg, said they would favor another stay.

Foster's accomplice in the murder, Shelton Ward, died of brain cancer on death row in 2010. Foster maintained in his trial that Ward acted alone and that contact between him and the victim was consensual.

218

The two men and Pal were regulars at Fat Albert's bar in Fort Worth when, the night before Valentine's Day in 2002, bartenders said Pal walked out with them, according to the report. Pal left in her car and the men followed closely behind in Foster's truck.

Eight hours later, Pal's body was found with a gunshot wound to the head and wadded-up duct tape nearby, according to the report.

Foster is the 30th person executed in the United States this year and the ninth in Texas.

In his last statement, Foster sent his love to his family and friends. "I love you, I pray one day we will all meet in heaven...," Foster said. "Ready to go home to meet my maker."

Texas has executed more than four times as many people as any other state since the death penalty was reinstated in the United States in 1976, according to the Death Penalty Information Center.

(Writing by Greg McCune; Editing by Mary WisniewskiandBillTrott)
http://www.reuters.com/article/2012/09/26/us-usa-texas-execution-confirmation-idUSBRE88P01D20120926

HIS OFFICIAL LAST STATEMENT:

Yes, you know I sat in my cell many days wondering what my last words would be: love for my family, grandson, friends. I love you very much. Tonight, when I close my eyes, I'll be with my Father. Some time ago I got a letter, I read it, and stuck it in with a bunch of stuff; and I thought to myself, what a cold-hearted person. I was asked about the letter, I spent half the night looking for the letter. A little part of the letter touched me. Over the years, I have learned to love. God is everything. God is my life. Tonight, I will be with Him. I am a parent myself. I have so much for this dear lady. I understand where they're coming from, I thought every person was cruel. I love you so, Susan. You know what it is girl, love ya. Maurie, appreciate it girl. Much love to you all. Mrs. Cox, love you. Momma, you are my hero. I wish this world was just like you. Another mother got hurt, as a parent I understand the pain. That letter she wrote wasn't wrong, she was just hurting. She showed God's love for letting me know that love will be there to welcome me home. I love you all. I don't know what you are going to feel after tonight. I love you. I pray one day we will all meet in heaven. A man told me 11 years ago the hardest thing to say is, "I forgive you." Hope one day we all be together again. I love you all: Susan, Mrs. Cox, momma, Maurie, Michael. Grandbabies make the world go around. I love you all. Warden, I am looking to leave this place on wings of a homesick angel. Ready to go home to meet my maker. What a friend we have in Jesus, oh my God, I lay in awe 'cause I love you, God. I love you, momma. I love you, Susan.

BROJACK'S FINAL COMMENTS:

It took eight years, five months, twenty-five days, four requests for stays of execution (three successful), and four trips to the execution chamber for my friend Sarge to finally be executed. We continued to talk almost weekly until September 25, 2012. Was Sarge guilty? I do not know, but I do know this. The next time we meet, there will be no steel doors or bars separating us! Amen?

May the grace of the Lord Jesus Christ be with God's people. Amen.

Revelation 22:21

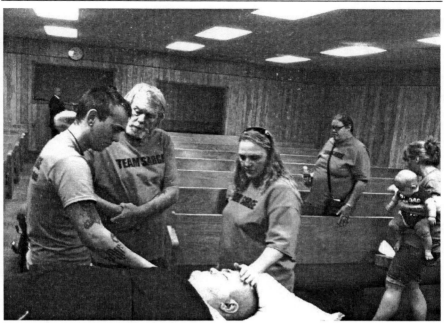

The State of Texas has a policy that allows family members to visit the body of an inmate immediately after they are executed. The body is moved to a chapel and family members have an opportunity to say goodbye. This is Sarge's son saying his final goodbye. It does not get any more real that this!

WWW.BROJACKMINISTRIES.COM

BROJACK@BROJACKMINISTRIES.ORG

COPIES AVAILABLE AT:
www.amazon.com
www.barnesandnoble.com
www.createspace.com